MISERABLE
Bitches
AND
Bastards

**Are you really miserable?
And, what you can do about it!**

WILLIAM J. MORIN

©2018 William J. Morin

All rights reserved.

For information contact:
William J. Morin
bmorin@wjmassoc.com

Printed in the U.S.A.

Disclaimer: All of the stories in the book are from my personal experiences and are based on actual counseling sessions with top leaders from various organizations. However, some of the descriptions of the participants have been changed to protect their identities.

MISERABLE *Bitches* AND Bastards

— ACKNOWLEDGMENTS —

As the author of *Miserable Bitches and Bastards*, it is a great pleasure for me to recognize a man who contributed greatly to the conceiving and writing of this book.

Mark Misercola is a successful writer, professor, and business executive who assisted me "every step of the way." Mark is a rare and wonderful person who is brilliant and egoless, all in one. Most of all, he is my friend who assisted me with his ability to observe without judging. A rare person, indeed!

I want you, the reader, to know of his role in getting this book completed.

William J. Morin

Dedication

*To my three sons, Mark, Timothy and Jason, and
four wonderful grandchildren, Knicole, Jaiden, Ivy and Ashby,
and a very special person – Brianna – all of whom
have taught me unconditional love.*

— FOREWORD —

After forty years of counseling executives in all kinds of organizations and corporations, it is still amazing to me how often business leaders are described by their subordinates and peers as being real bitches or bastards. As a counselor, I was frequently asked by clients (including CEOs and many company boards) to find out what these individuals might be doing to cause so many subordinates, peers, and, in some cases, even bosses to refer to them in these terms. Many times I would find out that these leaders thought they were doing the right job by being tough, insulting, or insensitive all so that they could get the overall job done.

This kind of behavior got them to where they were, and it was why they were known as tough, single-minded, and get-the-job-done-at-all-costs people. But as they rose through the ranks and gained more and more subordinates and power, no one ever told them they needed to try something else besides fear and chastisement to motivate people.

In the final analysis, however, most leaders who make it to the very top employ more of a conciliatory "let me listen" style of management with those they manage and serve. We have called this book *Miserable Bitches and Bastards* because it represents our hope that for both women and men this style of management has come and gone!

Numerous blank pages are available throughout this book for you to take notes and record insights that you may want to make about yourself as you go through the reading of the book.

— TABLE OF CONTENTS —

Concept and Biography 1

Introduction 7

Chapter I: The Journey 13

Chapter II: How Miserable Are You? 21

Chapter III: What the Hell is it All About? 27
Getting Honest with Yourself

Chapter IV: Defining Miserable 37

Chapter V: The Test 43

Chapter VI: Being Important— 53
Does That Make Us Miserable or Happy?

Chapter VII: Why Does Termination and Retirement 59
Frighten Us So Much?

Chapter VIII: Is the Price of Success Too High? What Is Too High? 65

Chapter IX: Climbing Out of the Misery Pit: 83
Is There an Answer to "How Do I Become Less Miserable
or Even Become Happy?"—Yes!

Chapter X: Megan's Story—What Does It Mean to Be Successful? 93

Chapter XI: The "Click" of the Moment 103

Chapter XII: No Dogmatic Thinking 107

Chapter XIII: To Serve "Is" One of the Answers—Servant Leadership 113

Chapter XIV: Yes, There Is an Answer 121

— CONCEPT AND BIOGRAPHY —

There is no shortage of depressing news in our world today, including opioid addictions, school shootings, divorce rates at all-time highs, global warming, politicians doing nothing, Russia meddling in our presidential election, and a general lack of ethics—a word that seems to mean absolutely nothing—across the business and political spectrum. Is it any wonder so many of us are miserable?

There are many reasons to be miserable. However, ultimately, each and every one of us controls our own individual "miserable button." Learning how to manage that button has become increasingly difficult for many of us, given the onslaught of depressing news and information that we are bombarded with every day. If anything, as social media has become so central to our lives, it's becoming harder and harder to not be depressed and miserable when you consider all the forces that are facing us at the moment.

Being unhappy about what you do and how you deal with it is not a new challenge! In fact, it is as old as mankind. Nevertheless, we seem to have a responsibility to be content with what we have. So many people hang in there due to tradition, the expectations of others, or even their religions. They hang on to jobs, marriages, and relationships that make them miserable, and wake up one day in their golden years approaching retirement being very, very unhappy. Without treatment, being miserable can quickly become debilitating. Okay, so why be miserable?

Several years ago, I was asked by publisher HarperCollins to write a proposal for a book about how miserable many of the world's top business and professional leaders had become. At the time, as CEO of Drake Beam Morin, Inc., which was the world's largest Outplacement firm, I was fortunate to have a front-row seat on the mental health attitudes and well-being (or lack thereof) of many of the day's most senior leaders. The problem was bad enough for profit and nonprofit organizations that HarperCollins entitled the working draft, "Miserable Bastards." Because women were becoming leaders in every

Miserable Bitches and Bastards

aspect of life, I later added "Bitches" to the title. Hence, the title *Miserable Bitches and Bastards*. With a wealth of real-life and statistical material to draw from, I started developing a manuscript that looked at why many accomplished leaders, both men and women, were becoming so increasingly unhappy and falling into what I call the "misery pit."

For me, business priorities and some personal health issues caused me to put the manuscript down for a while. But the concept of a book stuck with me. Now I have more time on my hands, and I have revisited my proposal and concluded that this topic is more relevant than ever, mainly because today's leaders—both men and women—are even more unhappy, unsatisfied, and unfulfilled than they were before the financial crisis of 2008 and the subsequent Great Recession.

While this idea goes counter to conventional wisdom, when you hear these leaders' stories about how little they were able to achieve in their command chairs of power, and how desperately they were searching for solutions, you will understand why this book is so necessary. In its original form, it was intended for an audience of senior executives who were primarily male. This is no longer the case. Therefore, this is a book about (and intended to assist) a new generation of male and female leaders from all walks of life whose accomplishments have left them asking, "Is this all there is?"

This book also targets the legions of disenchanted corporate and organizational leaders who have had enough; those who are saying "the personal price I have paid (or am paying) for the success I've attained (or am trying to attain) is simply too high and not worth pursuing anymore."

The first half of the book examines the causes that lead many successful people to a highly miserable existence. The second half shows what those people can do to regain a sense of career purpose and passion, and move to a stage where they feel really good about their endeavors.

What will be gained from reading this book? Much as I would like to say there is a magic solution for the miserable state in which many leaders find themselves, I can't. Every situation is different, and it is important to

William J. Morin

remember that regaining or attaining a sense of well-being is a process, not an event. While I am not a philosopher or even a professor, I too have been down this path and can say with certainty, "I've been there" and "I've done that." And with that perspective in mind, I can offer readers real insights and a plan for regaining their balance and sense of personal fulfillment.

Miserable Bitches and Bastards will show with certainty that the path to greater happiness is filled with many exciting options, including one that I call Servant Leadership, which involves leading, serving, protecting, and caring for others in a way that most management books do not even mention.

Sincerely,

William J. Morin
Founder, WJM Associates, Inc.

William J. Morin
Founder, WJM Associates, Inc.

William (Bill) J. Morin was born in Kankakee, Illinois. He did well academically and received a scholarship to attend Southern Illinois University, where he majored in social sciences. He became student body president, was an honor cadet in the Air Force ROTC program, and was selected to work in the Peace Corps by then president John F. Kennedy.

Today, Bill is a recognized world leader in the Human Resources consulting industry. He has developed many effective Human Resources management strategies for Fortune 500 corporations over the past thirty years. In addition, during the course of his career, he has counseled countless executives and leaders, helping them make strategic choices in their careers and for managing their businesses.

For more than twenty years, Bill was chairman and CEO of Drake Beam Morin, Inc., the world's leading organizational and individual transition consulting firm. Under his leadership, the firm grew from one office with sales of under $1 million in 1976 to an international company with a network of more than 160 offices and revenues exceeding $225 million.

In 1996, Bill started WJM Associates, Inc., a management consulting business specializing in executive development. WJM Associates, Inc., consists of the following divisions: WJM Partners (executive coaching), WJM Executive Search™, WJM Assess™ (assessment), Fast Start™ (assimilation coaching), and Career Transition and Executive Team Building. He has personally worked with companies such as IBM, AT&T, General Motors, Merrill Lynch, Kodak, and more than two hundred of the Fortune 500 corporations on Human Resources management issues.

In addition, Bill has authored and co-authored books and articles about conducting successful staff reorganizations, corporate trust, job search techniques, coping with job loss, and corporate revitalization issues. A recent book, Total Career Fitness, published by Jossey-Bass, has been reviewed favorably by Fortune magazine, as well as by many other journals, and is currently in its fourth edition. Prior to this, he wrote *Trust Me* (DBM Publishing). He has also co-authored several books including

What Every Successful Woman Knows (McGraw-Hill); *Truth, Trust, and the Bottom Line* (Dearborn Publishing); *Driving the Career Highway* (Thomas Nelson); *Dismissal* (Harcourt/HBJ); and *Outplacement Techniques: A Positive Approach to Terminating Employees* (American Management Association).

Bill has been a frequent guest on network television and is quoted often in the business press. His network appearances have been on such programs as *Good Morning America*, *Today*, CNN's *Pinnacle*, *ABC Nightly News*, and *The NewsHour with Jim Lehrer*. He is also a frequent speaker to organizations interested in developing their executives and building effective leadership teams.

After receiving his master's degree from Southern Illinois University, Bill began his corporate career at General Foods Corporation, continued as director of sales at Cole National Corporation, and then served as director of field operations for Avon Products, Inc. Before that time, he was a teacher in Murphysboro and Kankakee, Illinois, in the field of social sciences.

After spending several years at Avon Products, Bill decided to join Drake, Beam Associates in New York City, where he worked to build the company into an international corporation.

In addition to his wide-ranging business interests, Bill has been involved in a variety of charitable and philanthropic activities, serving on the board of the United Earth Foundation and volunteering to help New York City's underprivileged. He is also an Ellis Island award winner and a supporter of the East Harlem School of Exodus House. In the last year, he has started supporting the St. Labre Indian School in Ashland, Montana.

Several years ago, he was especially honored to be named Corporate Leader of the Year by the National Women's Economic Alliance Foundation in Washington, D.C. He is a past board member of International Corporate Communications, Inc., a Human Resources software company.

Bill is currently working as a major supporter of JobsyWobsy, a nonprofit organization that helps young people discover and attain career success.

Miserable Bitches and Bastards

Introduction

"Miserable"! What a crummy word. Unfortunately, it describes all of us from time to time. Unfortunately, it is becoming most of the time for many of us. And, the condition carries plenty of other emotional baggage with it—"overly ambitious," "driven," "confused," and even "depressed" (oh God, depressed!) are a few other words that come to mind. It has been reported that twenty million Americans alone are mildly depressed. What the hell is "mildly depressed"?

We are all searching for happiness and meaning in our lives. Really? Maybe not you. Is it in our nature to want to succeed and do better for ourselves and our loved ones? Perhaps. There is nothing wrong with that, is there? To succeed, most of us have to lead or try to be leaders. It is the natural progression—moving up to where the big money is at the top. However, some of us are driven by unhappy childhoods, some by a competitive desire to be better than everyone else, some by a fear of failure, and some because of where we come from and the times in which we live. But, regardless of the reasons, somewhere along the way "living happily ever after" has become more than just an aspiration; it is an obsession. The end goal has been replaced by the thrill of the chase, and "happily ever after" has been supplanted by "financial security at all costs," and a "CYA" (cover your ass) mentality above all else!

Several prominent studies and numerous surveys point to the same conclusion—we are not as happy as we once were, and the likelihood is we will not be as happy a year from now as we are now. Even at the very top, there is widespread unhappiness. More CEOs—both new and tenured—were fired in 2017 than in any year since 2008. Why? Part of it is because top business leaders are under more pressure to perform than ever. And when they do not perform, more often than not, they're out. In the past two decades, 30 percent of Fortune 500 CEOs have lasted fewer than three years. The average tenure of a chief executive is now 7.6 years worldwide compared with 9.5 years in 1995. The *Harvard Business Review* reports that two out of five CEOs fail in their first eighteen months on the job.

Miserable Bitches and Bastards

Various consulting studies hint at the collateral damage—a 2014 report from the strategy-consulting arm of PricewaterhouseCoopers found that this lack of preparedness is costing an average of $1.8 billion in foregone shareholder values at companies that find themselves dealing with forced turnovers at the top. In addition, as always, it is the shareholders who foot the bill. The same report found that "median shareholder return at companies that have changed CEOs falls to −3.5% (relative to the index they trade on) in the year after the change."

We are seeing this play out on a number of levels today. One significant contributor to senior executive turnover is that in today's increasingly difficult environment, CEOs, presidents, and other top officers have fewer and fewer individuals who they can trust to openly discuss organizational concerns with. They often lament the "lack of agenda-free confidants" available on their boards or management teams, given the inherent adversarial nature of boss/subordinate relationships. Social media has contributed to a prevailing attitude that says, "Never trust anyone in corporate life." Maybe the correct attitude is "Never trust anyone." What a nasty way to live!

Some of it is a function of the times. Though the global economy has improved recently, many of us are still recovering emotionally from the impact of the Great Recession. By all accounts, it was as economically gut-wrenching an experience as we have seen since the Great Depression in 1929, which left plenty of emotional scars in its wake. But the root problem behind what is troubling many senior leaders goes much deeper than economic cycles. We continue to look for happiness in all the wrong places, starting with money and all of its trappings.

Do you remember the old Warner Brothers cartoon where a delirious Daffy Duck suddenly finds himself filthy rich after being granted three wishes from a genie who has been freed from his magic lamp? Daffy's response is priceless: "Oh boy, oh boy, I'm rich! I'm wealthy! I'm independent! I'm socially secure!" But eventually, as we all know, no amount of wealth is enough. And when Daffy decides to sell the magic lamp to make even more money, he is warned by the angry genie, "Prepare to take the consequences" for desecrating the spirit of the lamp. Do you remember Daffy's next response? "Consequences schmonsequences . . . as long as I'm rich."

These are fitting words for a generation that has been obsessed with obtaining wealth at any cost, regardless of the consequences. And indeed, part of our prevailing attitude today is that happiness will follow the trail of money. Daffy follows the trail and pays the ultimate price. The genie transforms him into a miniature duck, and in an instant he becomes both a symbol and a victim of his own single-minded obsession.

Many of us find ourselves at a similar juncture today. We have "chased" financial success. We have moved up the career ladder. We have accumulated many things—cars, boats, homes, and properties. Yet, the more wealth we have amassed the unhappier we seem to have become. Think about it. How many times have you said to yourself, "If only I had had that promotion" or "If only I could have made it to CEO" or "If only I could build a vacation home" or "If only I could buy that dream car . . . I'd be truly happy." And how many times have you discovered that once you achieved your impossible dream you were more miserable than or as miserable as you were before the attainment? Never? Come on . . . be honest!

We would all do well to remember the words of the late Bill Cunningham, an outstanding New York Times fashion photographer who would rip up paychecks and say, "Money's the cheapest thing. Liberty and freedom are the most expensive!"

This reminds me of a friend of mine with whom I went to college. He was in this very same boat. All he cared about was making money; he constantly spoke about money as a major measure of success. In college, he had suffered an injury to his left leg and, even at twenty-three years old, often had to use a cane to walk around. That did not stop him from dreaming about and pushing for money, however. Nor did he hesitate to tell everyone around him that money made the difference in life, even though he would curse the cane he had to lean on for support.

After many years our friendship withered because I had discovered there were many experiences and moments that produced a sense of well-being that money had very little to do with. Yet, when we would meet once or twice a year, his theme of making money was secure and present. He still

Miserable Bitches and Bastards

spoke of money even though now that he was in a wheelchair. One could offer the thought that perhaps money was a strong motivation that kept him going in spite of all his physical ailments. But I also did not find him interesting enough to share ideas on how we might improve our careers, our children's educational status, or our marriages or even his own health.

He still maintained that money was the only thing that was real in life. However, he did finally admit that he was extremely miserable. Repeatedly he asked me what I thought because I was one of his oldest friends. I told him repeatedly there was more to life than money, and I used the example of his youngest son, who was facing an immobilizing illness that had resulted from a car accident. His son could not walk. I finally asked my friend one day, "Would you give up all your money if it would help your son walk again?" It took him an inordinate amount of time to say yes.

If you find yourself identifying with being in a similar situation or are aware of all of the above, you are not alone. I have been there too. I have run major corporations. Or, they ran me! I have attained wealth, power, and status. On the way up the ladder of success, I was driven by an unwavering belief that if I just kept pushing forward, I would have it made, and everything would be bigger and better and more fulfilling. But when I finally reached the mountaintop, it wasn't anything like I thought it would be. I found that success came at the cost of personal relationships, my health, and self-confidence Like many other successful executives, I had become a soldier among the ranks of *"les corporate misérables"* —a true life, red-blooded American who worked like mad, who was constantly and absolutely sure that success was defined by wealth and power attainment, and was absolutely, totally miserable. I thought, with no pain there is no gain.

You say that's too negative and too miserable to contemplate. You say it's not "that" bad. Really?

Hence, the premise for this book. *Miserable Bitches and Bastards* is about those (and to assist those) whose accomplishments have left them confused, empty, and, yes, miserable. Who are they? Perhaps they are you! It would be tempting to say, "You know who you are," but that is not always the case. If you're thumbing through this book, you may suspect something is wrong. But if you are like most of us, you're not exactly sure why you are so miserable, down, turned off, ill at ease, or just not right. And chances are you've been asking yourself the very common question "Is this all there is?" If you are asking these questions and do not have answers, you have come to the right place. As stated before, this book is for the legions of disenchanted corporate and organizational leaders who say they have had enough; those who are saying "the personal price we've paid (or are paying) for the success we've attained (or are trying to attain) is simply too high." If you are saying or feeling this, good for you. You are on your way to real success.

The first half of this book examines the causes that lead many of us to highly miserable existences. The second half shows what you can do about it; how you can regain a sense of purpose and passion, and how you can move to a stage where you feel really good about life. You are right ... it sounds like BS but *hang in there!*

What will you gain from reading this book? Much as I would like to say there is a magic solution for the miserable state many of us find ourselves in, I can't! Every personal situation is different, and it is important to remember as we have said before, that regaining or attaining a sense of well-being is a process, not an event.

Are you miserable? Let's find out ...

Miserable Bitches and Bastards

Chapter 1

Miserable Bitches and Bastards

Chapter I: The Journey

What is it all about? It is a question that has continually fascinated me. In my golden years, I have all that a man could ask for in life: great sons, each of whom I love "unconditionally." They have created in me a level of love that I could not have experienced without each of them. I have had an absolutely first-class career experience and have many, many friends whom I cherish. My health is about as average as you might expect for someone in his golden years. But, overall, I'm okay and it is what it is!

So what the hell is "it" all about? It must be passion. Passion is defined as a headless, non-evaluating drive toward an "all-consuming" focus, belief, or goal." Wow, what a definition of what it is "all" about. Sounds like BS!

Maybe it is! Maybe it is bits and pieces of headlines; an unconditional emotion we call love—that sensation you feel when you think you love something or someone at all levels of being alive.

Have you noticed that the news is mostly negative? How many associates and friends say "life is just wonderful" when they are asked the simple question "How are you doing?" Maybe 5 percent actually mean it. Do you really care?

Shouldn't our lives and our news be balanced with some positive information? Or is it always "that" bad? Aren't we all afraid to ask most people how they are? Did you ever notice when you say, "How are you?" that we hardly ever expect or want a positive or a negative response? Do we really, really care about how someone feels? Do we really have or take the time to listen for a response?

So, what is the point? Are we really so self-centered that we are truly miserable men and women UNLESS we are talking about what "we" need to make ourselves happy?

Miserable Bitches and Bastards

The old saying that "misery loves company" is at least partially true for me. I was compelled to write this book because of my own struggles with this issue. At one time, I headed a multimillion-dollar organization; I had achieved a level of success that exceeded anything I had ever aspired to and I had every reason in the world to be happy. But after you read my story, the last word anyone would apply to me is "happy." In fact, at the very peak of my career, I was quite successfully miserable. Fortunately, that is not the case today, as I have regained a sense of satisfaction, balance, and happiness in my life. But as we begin this examination of career misery, a closer, first-person look at my story and what caused so much misery for me is a worthy place to start.

Over a five-year period in the mid-1970s, whatever we touched at our company, Drake Beam Morin, turned to gold. We were really cranking, because we were essentially the first company to develop worldwide Outplacement services, and we were the best game in town for assisting those employees who had just lost their jobs. We were the CBS News of Outplacement and were up against a company called Thomas Hubbard, Inc. (THIK), which was very small. We, on the other hand, had all the firepower of a parent company behind us, and we were also very lucky because we were putting up offices all over the world and they were turning profitable right away. We were all over the Human Resources trade publications. In addition, we had high-profile clients like Bristol-Myers Squibb, Allied Signal, IBM, General Electric, and General Motors, all saying great things about us and recommending us to other organizations.

It was apparent that we were going to make more money as a subsidiary than any other group of businesses in the parent company. Our leaders of DBM had earned the right to have company cars and very high bonuses. But instead of celebrating, I was informed one day out of the blue that the chairman and CEO of our parent firm was not going to accept such "opulence" in the company. The bonuses and company cars would be removed from our subsidiary.

My first thought was, if they take these immediate "perks" away, we will be sued and I will lose the company. My boss, a vice chairman, said, "Let the legal beagles handle it. Don't get involved." I said no. I could not do that, not because I am noble but because it would cost too much for all the lawyers and my team would revolt and leave, look for new jobs, and no one would ever trust us again.

As I looked at the compensation/bonus plan, there was no caveat that said management could change the plan if they wanted. However, there was also no caveat that said management couldn't do this. Altering a bonus plan midterm just wasn't done in those days unless the company was doing poorly. We were new on the success block, and we were building the team in a very solid way. I did not want to face this catastrophe. Word got out about what our parent was going to do, and over the next two-month period I felt like I was getting slammed by my management on one side, and by my own subordinates on the other. My subordinates had heard rumors about the changes and were threatening to quit en masse. It turned out that my own boss, the vice chairman, had let the cat out of the bag by talking to several of my direct reports.

Here we were, this successful subsidiary that was generating all this money, and the big boys, who were more concerned about publishing books, were destroying my company without thinking of the consequences.

So against my direct boss's advice, I sent the chairman a letter begging him to reconsider the "takeaway." Finally, he agreed to meet with me. My boss said the chairman would be conciliatory and supportive. I had been miserable for months and I was desperate for relief. At that point, I just wanted it over with—I wanted out. The pressure was mounting, I had been traveling a great deal, and I was exhausted.

The day arrived and the meeting was scheduled at 1:30. The chairman kept me waiting for about fifteen minutes. I remember his assistant would not speak to me or look at me, which was not a good sign. Finally, the door opened. The leader, who was my height (six-foot-four), came out and handed the assistant something and said to me, "Okay, you can get in here now." I walked into this huge, imposing office. In the middle of the room, he turned to me, face-to-face and man to man, and said, "Who the fuck do you think you are?" It caught me so off guard that I literally did not know at that

Miserable Bitches and Bastards

moment who the fuck I was! Here I was with the chairman of a $4 billion company, with an office bigger than God's (I think), and I certainly did not want to be there under those conditions.

I think I responded in a squeaky voice, "I guess we're going to find out." He snapped back, "I've had enough of you." He said, "Sit down! I have to put up with you and I have to hear about your success all the time. I have to worry about Joe. Joe works around the clock, he is my protégé, and you're making more money than he does. It's just abominable."

Joe, a very good and capable ex-football coach, somehow had gotten into the boss's good graces. But I really didn't know him or anything about what he did. We were now sitting down across his desk from each other.

Then suddenly the chairman grabbed a tub of pencils on his desk—pointy ends up—and screamed, "I've had enough!" and slammed the tub of pencils down with enough force that several shot out of their container and flew around the room. One flew past my face like an arrow and stuck in the philodendron plant right next to me.

I became enraged. I stood up and walked around the desk, raised my arm, and fully intended to punch his lights out. I was literally out of my mind. I called him an SOB. He said, "You're going to hit me." And I said, "Yes, sir!"

His eyes got as wide as footballs and something—a little voice inside—stopped me and I realized that I was dealing with a completely crazy man. So I backed away and sat back down. Then he actually asked me, "Why do you need the cars and bonuses?" as if he had other things on his mind. I said, "We'll lose our key people." I didn't say I'll lose "my" people, I said "our" people. "All right," he said, "you can have them. And keep the bonus plan. You're doing a great job."

Just like that, the deal was done. He walked around the desk, put his arm around me, and walked me to the door. "I'm glad we have an understanding about this," he said.

William J. Morin

So my story had a happy ending because we got to keep our perks. The chairman retired several years later and Drake Beam Morin continued to grow all around the world.

But the entire time that I worked under that type of management I was incredibly miserable. I had no support from management. We knew back then that Outplacement was a recessionary phenomenon. We knew we needed to go into other consulting services, but we needed our parent company to allow us to take some of our profits to do this. Whenever I would mention these development areas to management above me, management would say, "Stick to your knitting!" We did! It made me miserable and it affected virtually every aspect of my life—work, family, you name it. When you work for someone who does not care, eventually you stop caring. Like many other successful executives, I was very "successfully miserable."

Miserable Bitches and Bastards

Chapter II

Miserable Bitches and Bastards

Chapter II:
How Miserable Are You?

Not so long ago, a man, sixty-three years of age, was sitting in my office saying, "I got $20 million in the bank but it's not enough to make me feel right." I asked, "Don't you feel all right?" He responded, "You know, it doesn't make me feel happy about my life and my future."

A woman sitting in the same chair about two days later said, "I have been working for nine years, but everyone hates me and probably always did hate me. I am so miserable. Can you believe it? People really hate me!"

A day later, a thirty-four-year-old woman making two hundred thousand dollars a year and hated her job was sitting in the same chair. "You don't understand," she said, when I asked her why she hated her job. "I really, really hate my job. I'm ready to lose my life altogether. I am the most miserable person I know. I wanted to be married with kids and all I get in life is this stinking job."

Finally, three days later, a young man said, "I am just miserable, and all I want is to not be miserable."

All of these driven individuals who were climbing the "ladder of success" are gone—retired or dead. On the surface, each one could have been described as fulfilling the American Dream. At the time, they were all working hard, making a lot of money, and were good at what they were doing. There are many executives today who might be willing to trade places with them. Yet, they were all completely miserable. What about you? Do you really like what you are doing?

They (and maybe you) are why I have written this book and titled it *Miserable Bitches and Bastards*. It is a shocking title for a shocking condition. I could have called this book *Poor Miserable Bitches and Bastards*, but the truth is many of the professionals who are featured in this book are anything but

Miserable Bitches and Bastards

poor. They have ascended to the very top of their professions and organizations. And they exemplify, in almost every sense of the word, "success." However, many have discovered that success, like money, isn't buying them happiness.

Who are these miserable bitches and bastards? "They" are the growing legions of disenchanted corporate and organizational leaders and employees who say they have had enough. What "they" are saying often sounds like this: "The personal price for the success we've attained (or are trying to attain) is simply too high and not worth pursuing." As a result, "they" are not only miserable, they are turned off and opting out of the corporate rat race at a higher and higher rate.

What is behind it? Some say we live in a world that wants "instant gratification." Others say it has come about because we are suffering from a "leadership crisis." Some feel it stems from a lack of "ethical" behavior. Others feel it has come about because many top corporate and organizational officers today simply lack the management skills they need to balance personal success and professional satisfaction. Some say greed is our new religion.

There is no lack of evidence. All of the above are probably true.

Time magazine, in a 2013 cover story entitled "The Pursuit of Happiness," reported that since 2004, the share of Americans who identify themselves as optimists has plummeted from 79 percent to 50 percent. An accompanying poll found fewer people are doing constructive things like helping others or praying/meditating to improve their moods. But people are spending more time on social media, even though 60 percent say they do not feel better about their lives.[1]

In this new age of uncertainty and anxiety, we have turned to pills, and self-improvement products and services, including books and seminars with motivational speakers. Yet, we are still an unhappy lot. In fact, a 2012 World Happiness Report, published by the Earth Institute of Columbia University, ranks the United States twenty-third on a fifty-country happiness index, far behind the happiest countries on earth—Iceland, New Zealand, and Denmark.[2]

Whatever the cause, many have good reason to feel the way they do. Because of their tremendous pay, perceived power, and seemingly aloof behavior, business and political leaders today are mistrusted as never before by subordinates, employees, and the public alike. Many associate public and business leaders with the "perp walk" images we've grown accustomed to seeing on the nightly news—that of common criminals being led off to jail in handcuffs or to the courthouse for trial. Cooking the books, lying to shareholders, denying guilt, and so on have become routine occurrences—or just "a day at the office"—for some corporate executives.

At the time of the writing of this book, the Parkland school shootings in Florida had just occurred. In its wake, many found a system that had failed to protect the students at virtually every level—from security procedures to the police response to ignored warnings of the gunman's intentions, to confused and polarized political leaders. All the systems that were in place to prevent and stop just such an incident from occurring failed.

Yet the bad news does not end here. Today's misery in the C-Suite is almost certain to beget more misery down the road for all of us. This looming crisis will center on the next generation of leaders—aspiring young executives and leaders who are watching it all unfold with skeptical eyes. Given what they are seeing, is it fair to ask who and what caliber of person would want leadership jobs in the future?

The early returns are not promising. The allure of leadership is fading. Many companies and organizations are already seeing the evidence in their own internal surveys. Younger employees are increasingly unwilling to sacrifice their free time and family lives for a shot at the top. A recent Northwestern University study found that many younger employees want more balance and harmony in their lives. They say they do not want to live in a fishbowl. For many of them, money and prestige alone are no longer sufficient motivators.

So what is to become of our leaders? And if we're drawing from a smaller pool, will the quality and caliber of leadership suffer? This book carefully examines why so many leaders who have made it in life are so miserable and why, in essence, they fail.

Miserable Bitches and Bastards

After advising more than two hundred senior leaders —both women and men—in profit and nonprofit organizations, I have discovered what so many of these very successful executives have found to be so troubling about their jobs. Most of them agree that attaining a balanced, successful family life, along with a successful career, is the most challenging of all their endeavors. In essence, the real problem here is not managing a business. It is managing their lives so they can "have it all" in balance. Is it really an impossible goal? Maybe!

In this book, I will review the real-life experiences of those who've climbed the summit and have found the climb far less fulfilling than what it was cracked up to be. (The names have been changed to protect the innocent and not so innocent.)

To be sure, there are *Miserable Bitches and Bastards* in all fields, in every industry, and every business. My expertise in this arena comes from more than forty years of working with executives around the world.

It is important to remember, as stated before, that regaining a sense of happiness and balance is a process, not a single event. Discovering the solution is unique to every one of us. It is the journey of a lifetime, and I hope you will join me.

---

[1] *Time*, July 8/15, 2013, page 27.
[2] *Time*, July 8/15, 2013, page 27.

Chapter III

Miserable Bitches and Bastards

Chapter III:
What the Hell is it All About? Getting Honest with Yourself

On the surface, we try to explain what the "hell" it's all about by thinking of paychecks, pleasing others, being recognized, being important, being loved, and on and on. In the end, all of these factors fall miserably short of what it is all about for all of us.

That is not to say that there is not good and evil in the world, but how we approach life is still a mystery compared with how we have gotten here. We usually want to blame it on DNA, Mommy and Daddy, political leaders, educators, perhaps our brothers and sisters and our friends. Most of all, we want to defiantly blame it on someone else, not us.

World-class philosophers, both ancient and current, have attempted to answer these questions in extremely philosophical and esoteric ways. Nietzsche, a rather modern philosopher, once said, "Against boredom even gods struggle in vain." He simply felt that at the core of life is a state of boredom that causes us for some reason or another to not get what we deserve and want for ourselves.

Misery, as the saying goes, loves company. It does not care who you are or what you do. In fact, misery in one form or another has afflicted some pretty well-known and accomplished people over the years. They have all had plenty to say about what it is like to be miserable. Consider:

> "Happy people find a way to live with their problems, and miserable people let their problems stop them from living. Miserable people focus on the things they hate about their life. Happy people focus on the things they love about their life."
> —*Sonya Parker, American author*

Miserable Bitches and Bastards

"The secret of being miserable is to have leisure to bother about whether you are happy or not. The cure for it is occupation."
—George Bernard Shaw, Irish playwright

"A man's as miserable as he thinks he is."
—Seneca, Roman philosopher

"There is no more miserable human being than one in whom nothing is habitual but indecision."
—William James, American philosopher and psychologist

"We generally fancy ourselves more miserable than we are, for want of taking a true estimate of things; wherefore we fly into transports without reason, and judge of the happiness or calamity of human life, by false lights."
—Wellins Calcott, English author

"There is always more misery among the lower classes than there is humanity in the higher."
—Victor Hugo, French poet, novelist, dramatist

"It is seldom that the miserable can help regarding their misery as a wrong inflicted by those who are less miserable."
—George Eliot, English novelist

"The truly miserable have a timbre in their voices strong enough to erase smiles from the faces and souls of the contented."
—Saint Jerome, priest, theologian, and historian

"Oftentimes, when people are miserable, they will want to make other people miserable, too. But it never helps."
—Lemony Snicket, aka American novelist Daniel Handler

"The miserable have no other medicine. But only hope."
—William Shakespeare, English poet and playwright

"I've learned from experience that the greater part of our happiness or misery depends on our disposition and not on our circumstances."
—Martha Washington, America's first First Lady

"I stumbled out into the courtyard to try to flee my misery, but of course we can never flee the misery that is within us."
—Arthur Golden, American writer

"Some people are so addicted to their misery that they will destroy anything that gets in the way of their fix."
—Bryant McGill, American writer

"Part of every misery is, so to speak, the misery's shadow or reflection: the fact that you don't merely suffer but have to keep on thinking about the fact you suffer. I not only live each endless day in grief, but live each day thinking about living each day in grief."
—C. S. Lewis, English novelist

"The spendthrift robs his heirs, the miser robs himself."
—Jean de la Bruyere, French philosopher

"Maybe men are separated from each other only by the degree of their misery."
—Francis Picabia, French painter and poet

"All men's miseries derive from not being able to sit in a quiet room alone."
—Blaise Pascal, French mathematician, physicist, inventor, writer, and Catholic theologian

"A misery is not to be measured from the nature of the evil, but from the temper of the sufferer."
—Joseph Addison, English essayist, poet, and dramatist

Miserable Bitches and Bastards

"Depend upon it that if a man talks of his misfortunes there is something in them that is not disagreeable to him; for where there is nothing but pure misery there never is any recourse to the mention of it."
—Samuel Johnson, English writer

"No one is so miserable as the poor person who maintains the appearance of wealth."
—Charles Spurgeon, English preacher

"People talk about the courage of condemned men walking to the place of execution: sometimes it needs as much courage to walk with any kind of bearing towards another person's habitual misery."
—Graham Greene, English novelist

"A soul that is reluctant to share does not as a rule have much of its own. Miserliness is here a symptom of meagerness."
—Eric Hoffer, American writer and philosopher

"If someone makes you miserable more than they make you happy, it doesn't matter how much you love them, you need to let them go."
—Unknown

"We either make ourselves miserable, or we make ourselves happy. The amount of work is the same."
—Carlos Castaneda, American author and philosopher

"The happiest is the person who suffers the least pain; the most miserable who enjoys the least pleasure."
—Jean-Jacques Rousseau, French philosopher and writer

"[The] Miserable person lives without ideals,"
—Ivan Turgenev, Russian novelist

> "The miser, starving his brother's body, starves also his own soul, and at death shall creep out of his great estate of injustice, poor and naked and miserable."
> —*Theodore Parker, American theologian and scholar*

> "The contemplative life is often miserable. One must act more, think less, and not watch oneself live."
> —*Nicolas Chamfort, French writer*

Who among us can't see something of ourselves in these quotes? It seems to me that, in all candor, everything is related to our mind-set; what we believe at the moment. "I'm miserable, I'm not miserable." "I'm a failure, I'm successful." It is like gravity and antigravity, positive and negative energies, right and wrong, good and evil. The mind-set stays somewhere between the two poles. "I can't do that." "No one would ever expect me to do that, even though my mother told me that I should do that," or "I would like to do that, but I can't do that because . . ." Words like "I want," "I should," "I could," and "I can't" fill our daily vocabulary in a magnitude that we would be shocked at if we knew how often we actually use them. Words like "I wouldn't," "I can't," "I couldn't," "I never should," "No one would want me," "No one thinks I could do it," and on and on, fill our lives to the point of absurdity.

I have to quote President Trump at this point. He uses the first person ("I") more than any other leader I have ever observed. When we are using the word "I" with the world going to hell, we have to accept the responsibility for our causing the world to go to hell. Trump never speaks in a collective sense or in the third person. It is always "I did this," and "I did that."

People who are very miserable often say, "I wish I'd done this or that when I was younger." Or they comment, "I wish I had prepared myself for the current feelings that I have." In many ways, they are performing the greatest sin of living. That sin is "lying" to yourself. For example, it would be better to admit that you are frightened of feeling inadequate, and form an honest state in your mind of what your real challenges are, rather than lying to yourself about who you want to be and who you can be if you are really honest with yourself.

Miserable Bitches and Bastards

When you are honest with yourself, true healing can begin. Let's not fall back on excuses or dig too deeply into past failures. Simply stated, place a high value on yourself. Once you (and others) recognize this value, you tend to step out of the state of being miserable and begin to see yourself in a more honest and forthright reflection. Those who are depressed often speak about depression as being exhausting, that is, they have no energy to use toward life. Many people say if they work out/exercise during a state of depression or exhaustion, they feel better and exhilarated. Isn't it strange that when we are exerting energy, we feel better about ourselves and get even more energy? When you do nothing but complain, you get nothing but more misery.

Often people speak about what they wish they had done or become. I hear it all the time. "I wanted to be" a nuclear scientist or an astronomer with NASA or a top doctor. But they wake up one day, sixty-five years old with $20 million in the bank, and they feel like they have missed life all together. If you are really good at building a business, teaching a class, working with others, or working as a scientist, as Microsoft founder Bill Gates talks about so often, why not stay within the range of your talents and build on those talents until you have a sense of their value to you and to others. Gates has stated "unhappy customers are your greatest source of learning."

If you truly want to go on to become a nuclear scientist, you already know that it takes tremendous discipline and educational achievements. We call these "wish talents," the career equivalents of "I coulda," I shoulda," and "I woulda."

Wish talents make us more depressed and miserable. They are filled with regrets and remorse. They're sad reflections in a rearview mirror. Think of Marlon Brando when he says, "I coulda been a contender" in On the Waterfront. Natural talents build a sense of value and accomplishment when exercised and utilized for the benefit of others as well as ourselves.

Consider the story of thirty-one-year-old self-made millionaire Timothy Kim, who made a fortune on the stock market starting at age nineteen. Once he achieved his financial goal, he lacked a sense of purpose and became bored. In a recent interview with CNBC, he said, "People tend to think that they want this kind of lifestyle where they're on vacation for the rest of their life, and I actually disagree. I'm in this situation and I'm getting bored."

Kim's point: More money does not result in higher levels of happiness or a stress-free life. In fact, a LinkedIn study quoted in the CNBC story found that people who report making higher incomes tend to "face higher levels of stress at work and don't necessarily experience higher job satisfaction."

Kim's solution: He says rather than making wealth the end goal, you should focus on finding purposeful work that aligns with your passions. To avoid boredom, Kim runs his blog, gives financial advice, attends mentorship sessions to expand his knowledge, and collaborates with churches on philanthropic endeavors. "Human beings inherently want to do something more," he explains. "You want to use your mental capacity."

It is critical to value yourself and see how your talent fits in to contributing to society, as well as to your loved ones around you. Appreciating your value is the first step in getting out of the "miserable pit." You begin to sense value when people say, "Thank you," "I appreciate it," "You're wonderful," "You were helpful," "You did it," "You accomplished a lot." Many statements of appreciation slide by us and we don't place a very high level of appreciation on what those compliments could mean to making us feel more valuable and, hence, less miserable.

Miserable Bitches and Bastards

Chapter IV

Miserable Bitches and Bastards

Chapter IV: Defining Miserable

Most people who are miserable don't need a definition to figure out that they are miserable. Yet if you search "miserable" on the web, you will find literally thousands of definitions, synonyms, and quotes like these:

- Wretchedly unhappy, uneasy, or uncomfortable
- Wretchedly poor; needy
- Attended with or causing misery
- Manifesting misery
- Worthy of pity; deplorable

The Urban Dictionary defines "miserable" as "someone who is unhappy or unpleasant." And also describes it as "the feeling that we sometimes call depression without the attached social malaise (that is, the need to take medication, go to a shrink, talk too much, eat too much, et cetera)."

But as you read these definitions, the question you should ponder is: Do you see yourself in any of these?

A lot of us complain about being miserable/hopeless, but perhaps we are really not miserable. Maybe we complain about our lives, like the weather, but we do not expect much to happen in terms of being able to control or affect it in any meaningful way. Maybe "hopeless" is a better word than miserable.

However, for many of us, being miserable has become a way of life. Complain, complain, complain and one day we will awaken and find ourselves alone and often evaluated by others as a loser or incapable of leading, managing, or even getting along with our families, friends, and neighbors.

Miserable Bitches and Bastards

Newscasts, newspapers, most blogs, and magazine articles all describe, in detail, how miserable we are. A friend of mine once said, "we're broke, we're out of work, our 401(k) is a 101(k) or isn't doing as well as we think it should be, we don't have as much equity in our homes as we'd like, our school systems are dangerous and closing, and our health care system is all screwed up." In a recent survey, when asked to grade the U.S. government on its performance, the median grade was C–, and half of the three hundred thousand respondents gave Uncle Sam an F. All of these signs are telling us we are in a miserable state as a nation.

It is almost as if we have turned back the clock to 1976 and borrowed a scene from the movie Network. We are all "mad as hell" and we're "not going to take it anymore." Only, however, we do take it more.

It has come to the point where we should not be saying good morning to each other. We should really be asking, "How miserable are you today?" or "How pissed are you today?" or "How hopeless are you today?"

These are easy questions to ask but tough to answer. You really need to think them through. Is it an attitudinal challenge or is it really an attitudinal problem? Do you really see the glass half empty or half full? As with all things in life, self-analysis is the critical factor. In many cases, we just deny that we are miserable and that we need any assistance on any issues that may create a positive change in our lives. The very fact that you are reading this book is a definite step in the right direction. Being miserable may be defined as feeling down, feeling burned out, or feeling constantly negative. But you are recognizing you don't have to be miserable.

As stated before, we all agree that life is a journey and not just an event. However, we may all say we want our lives to be eventful. Life is, therefore, in fact, a process and we have limitless opportunities to affect the process in a positive way.

Are you miserable? Don't lie. Are you?

Many times when we are miserable, we blame the job, our organization, our coworkers, our products, and so on. In most cases, however, it is really not the job that is making us miserable but our careers. Many of us are frustrated that we have not achieved as much as we thought we would or moved up the career ladder the way we had envisioned when we started our careers.

In most cases, we tend to focus on our income or the job title, or that we do not have positions of impact and power. But those are short-sighted views. What should be important is that we feel like we are contributing to society, or making a difference for associates or subordinates and to the overall well-being of the organization. However, right now with all this being said, you might take the money and run.

Activities

One thing I strongly recommend is to write out a values statement involving your family, your job, your faith, and your career. What is your code of ethics? What do you value most? Write down your top ten or top five. This activity will help trigger questions in your mind so that you might "not" feel miserable or determine what is leading you to and making you feel miserable.

Here is my personal values list:

- To be honest with sensitivity.
- To think of the other person's motivation, needs, and desires first, before making judgments or even offering an observation.
- To concentrate on producing quality services or products with my work and leisure time, rather than self-serving activities.
- To take responsibility for all of my life's challenges and not blame my family members, friends, peers, the job, and so on.
- To persevere for the common good, no matter what the cost.

Why do we have you do this? Because we think you should show your code of ethics or values to everyone around you so that <u>they</u> might remind you from time to time that you seem to be off or really on in terms of what you

Miserable Bitches and Bastards

say you stand for. We have assisted corporations and organizations in writing their ethics codes, but often they hardly ever look at them again. What a waste of time!

Whether or not your job is making you miserable, what is making you feel even more miserable is that you feel powerless and perhaps that you cannot do anything about bringing about the changes that you want. Complete the code statement and see how you do. Ask others what they think about you and your "code of values."

The next activity is entitled "Is it your personal life?" These analysis steps are just thought starters in trying to get you to realize what might be making you miserable. However, most important, these analysis steps should cause you to start carefully determining the issues that you "can" control and that you can bring about change that can be positive for your life. Again, keep in mind, we are not talking about people who are bipolar, schizophrenic, or suffer from deep depression. These are conditions that need to be dealt with by professionals. We are talking about people who complain about being miserable but who seem not to want to do anything about their miserable status.

Please complete several questionnaires that follow, which should allow you to create a dialogue with a good friend or several friends about what is making you so miserable or feeling hopeless.

Chapter V

Miserable Bitches and Bastards

Chapter V: The Test

The following questions have been written by me, and I have used them when coaching others. They are not academically tested or certified. When the tests are complete and you have studied the results, we recommend that you speak with a "non-judgmental" friend about the reality of what you have discovered and see if he or she agrees. However, let's be careful here as to how we define a "friend."

A friend is someone who you have almost complete trust in and, most important, someone who is not quick to judge or give feedback. A true friend will listen to you, ask questions, and help "you" arrive at your own conclusions about what is making you miserable.

Friends help us analyze and work through life and agree that it is a journey, but they do not come up with pop psychology answers like those people we see on the Dr. Phil or Oprah TV programs. These people are all well and good, but a good friend is someone who helps us think through issues in a careful and objective way and to confront the various challenges we face in life.

So your "assignment" now is to chat with a good friend about what you discovered going through these steps about what might be making you miserable concerning your personal life and or your job.

What's Making Your Life Miserable? Is it Your Job?

	Always 1 pt	Frequently 2 pts	Occasionally 3 pts	Rarely 4pts	Never 5 pts
1. Do you wake up dreading the day and being in the organization's culture?					
2. Do you come home at the end of the day feeling physically and mentally exhausted?					
3. Do you feel like you are just going through the motions at work every day and are not really engaged in a meaningful way?					
4. Do you feel as if your direct supervisor is difficult and not supportive?					
5. Do you feel as if the people you work and interact with are difficult and unsupportive?					
6. Do you think you should leave this position if you had a better offer?					

	Always 1 pt	Frequently 2 pts	Occasionally 3 pts	Rarely 4 pts	Never 5 pts
7. Do you find it difficult to accomplish anything at work?					
8. Do you feel as if this position is everything you want it to be?					
9. Do you feel you are making a real contribution to your organization and society at large?					
10. Do you find yourself thinking, "What was I thinking?" when you aspired to this position?					

Total Score: _____

For the questions you have just answered, the lower the score the greater the likelihood your job is driving your misery.

If you scored …	It means …
10–20 points	Your job/career is definitely making you miserable.
21–30	Your job/career is not the only thing that is making you miserable, but it is a significant factor in your misery.
31–40	You are reasonably satisfied with your job/career.
41–50	You like what you are doing and where you are heading.

What is Making You Miserable? Is it Your Family?

	Always 1 pt	Frequently 2 pts	Occasionally 3 pts	Rarely 4pts	Never 5 pts
1. Do you dread going home at the end of the day?					
2. Do you find yourself making excuses to stay late at the office?					
3. Do you feel as if your family situation is out of control?					
4. Do you see your job as an escape from home?					
5. Do you dread weekends?					
6. Are you invigorated by your family or exhausted?					
7. Do you look forward to spending time with your spouse or significant other?					

	Always 1 pt	Frequently 2 pts	Occasionally 3 pts	Rarely 4pts	Never 5 pts
8. Do you and your spouse or significant other agree on most issues?					
9. Do you and your spouse or significant other disagree on most issues?					
10. Are you and your spouse or significant other a team working toward the same goals?					

Total Score: _____

For the questions you have just answered, the lower the score the greater the likelihood your family and/or relationship is driving your misery.

If you scored …	It means …
10–20 points	Your personal life is definitely making you miserable.
21–30	Your personal life is not the only thing that is making you miserable, but it is a significant factor in your misery.
31–40	You are reasonably satisfied with your personal life
41–50	Your personal life (family and relationship with your spouse or significant other) is strong and not the source of your misery.

What is Making You Miserable? Is it the Economy or Society?

	Always 1 pt	Frequently 2 pts	Occasionally 3 pts	Rarely 4pts	Never 5 pts
1. Do you find yourself obsessing over current public affairs?					
2. Do your moods swing with the ups and downs of the stock market?					
3. Do you constantly watch the all-news or business cable channels?					
4. Do you worry constantly about the economy? Our country?					
5. Are you worried about your own personal finances?					
6. Do you fear the future?					
7. Are you worried about the state of our country and its prospects?					

	Always 1 pt	Frequently 2 pts	Occasionally 3 pts	Rarely 4pts	Never 5 pts
8. Do you personalize every news report and worry about how it will affect you?					
9. Do you scrutinize your portfolio and bank accounts every day?					
10. Do you feel happy about your financial situation at this time?					

Total Score: _____

For the questions you have just answered, the lower the score the greater the likelihood your family and/or relationship is driving your misery.

If you scored ...	It means ...
10–20 points	Economic and societal conditions are definitely making you miserable.
21–30	Economic and societal conditions are not the only things that is making you miserable, but it is a significant factor in your misery.
31–40	When it comes to economic and societal conditions, you are reasonably satisfied.
41–50	The economy and society are not the root causes of your misery.

Miserable Bitches and Bastards

Chapter VI

Miserable Bitches and Bastards

Chapter VI:
Being Important—Does That Make Us Miserable or Happy?

Like everyone else in life, we all want to be important. As usual, this can be both negative and positive. Who among us doesn't want to be valued, liked, loved, and respected? Who doesn't want to be appreciated for our accomplishments and recognized for what we have done well? And at the same time, who doesn't want to be forgiven for what we have not done so well?

One could argue that our families have set the goals for us to attain certain levels of financial security, status, and influence over others. Maybe we can blame Mom and Dad, our grandparents, or siblings for forcing us to think in those ways of being powerful and important. Unfortunately, most of us feel that we have underachieved and, as a result, are not respected or recognized for what we stand for, what we think, and what we've accomplished. In this state of mind, we can become very miserable.

Once again, if we are being really honest with ourselves, we realize if we have or have not achieved certain accomplishments, or made certain decisions that have worked well for us. When we have that state of honesty with ourselves, we also know where we have failed; where we have not done the job, and have let down ourselves and those who believe in us.

Wanting to be important is often a driving force that can be very, very negative in how we operate with others. The need to be important is mixed with the idea of being powerful and having an answer before there are even questions. This drive to be powerful and important, and the mixture thereof, can make us appear, in reality, not to care about others. As they say on Broadway, the "roar of the crowd" drives us to search for power above all else.

It seems that truly humble people are happier and not driven by the need to be recognized or to hear laudatory comments about how wonderful they

Miserable Bitches and Bastards

are. Hence, wanting to be important is often a driving force that can work for evil and make us very, very miserable. Especially when we do not think we are attaining a certain position of power.

However, aspiring to success, power, and money can move us in another direction, the right direction—to give service to others—when we realize that we have to attain things in life so that we can contribute to the welfare of others. The danger of course is that the idea of building massive amounts of money or putting your name on the door of a facility, or a college or a company, or whatever can be debilitating. Even if we gain this kind of recognition, it can make us miserable because of what happens to our lack of achievements in the future. We can peak too early.

When someone achieves a certain level of importance, it is quite common for them to begin to ask, "Is that it?" We think, "Now that I have become the CEO, or the president, or the leader of the organization, what am I going to work on and do with the rest of my life?" And "How am I going to feel good about something else?" These questions often cause us to become very miserable because we do not have answers and we are shocked that we're not happier once we have attained an important position.

It is becoming quite popular to provide an on-boarding coach to C-level executives, presidents, or CEOs. As you know, all of these titles are given to people who have reached the top positions in a company. Often, there is a moment of confusion and almost "disarray" if the individual feels that he or she is not ready to take over the position. Donald Trump, our president, said that when he got off Air Force One and walked through the front door of the White House, he had a funny feeling that he was not prepared for what he was going to find on the other side of the door.

I think we have all had these almost surreal experiences where we feel like we are not where we actually are, especially when we are taking on greater responsibilities and have worked very hard to get where we are in life. I mean that. I have sometimes wondered, "How the hell did I get here?" and "What am I doing here?"

Recently, I was counseling an individual who had finally made it to the top position that he had been seeking. After literally years of work and being counseled by professionals like myself, the day arrived when he was going to take over a $200 million sales organization. As he arrived at the office that morning, he was experiencing all kinds of stresses, including forgetting the name of the receptionist who had been at her desk for more than ten years. He just could not remember her name, and now she was standing at attention as he walked through the door after hearing that he was going to be the new president. Sometimes, getting what we want can make us very skittish and, in fact, very miserable.

This individual felt he was not even aware of the skills that many of his staff members had, when all along he thought he knew. As he began to realize he was responsible for the development of their talents, as well as using those talents, he began to question himself more and more. Hence, self-doubt and questioning ourselves seems to go along with attainment of power. Most of us do not want to show that we are confused, fearful, and, indeed, feeling a little humble at having secured a position that maybe other people in the organization also definitely wanted.

In another case, I was counseling a woman who had moved around a number of people to get to the position of director and leader of the organization. Frankly, all of the people she had moved around resented her and that attitude toward her terrified her. In fact, after a year she was removed from the position because she could not put up with the negative thinking of her people.

Striving to be important is an extremely emotional process that can be very "off-putting" if you do not realize that all human beings go through these types of challenges when they take over leadership positions. Frankly, it would be better to think about how we are going to make a contribution to the organization when we are in a leadership role, rather than feeling a sense of being important to the company because we have been promoted. Contributing is far more meaningful and rewarding than simply being the leader.

Miserable Bitches and Bastards

Chapter VII

Miserable Bitches and Bastards

Chapter VII:
Why Does Termination and Retirement Frighten Us So Much?

Fear of failure haunts almost all of humanity. Nothing brings that home more than being terminated from a job or approaching the age of retirement when we know we have to leave what we have been doing for a long time. This challenge seems to frighten us all, and it is right up there with other demons—the fear that we are never going to become important, or successful, or wealthy, or well known. In fact, we know we are going to die!

After spending thirty years specializing in Outplacement Counseling, Retirement Counseling, Career Guidance, and all other aspects of career management challenges, I have seen many people face termination, job loss, retirement, company buyouts, and, ultimately, job or career change. In most cases, the individuals I dealt with were terrified over losing their jobs, a change in their job environment, or not being identified with their jobs anymore.

Psychologists tell us that insecurity is at the core of most human beings' attitudes. One psychologist defined insecurity to me one day as not feeling that we have accomplished anything in life. Therefore, when we are feeling this lack of accomplishment, we believe we are not of any value to society, to our families, or to ourselves. It is, in fact, very frightening to think we could live our lives and not have the recognition we wanted or expected to have when we were young. When our lives are ahead of us, we all have a tendency to think life will always be better, we will improve with time, and that wonderful, ultimate position "will be ours."

While we are in this state of mind that "things will always be better," we are not always aware of how good things already are, and we're not reaching out

Miserable Bitches and Bastards

to show our appreciation to others. We often think that around the bend in our own personal world things will improve more than we could realize, and we will be rewarded by having more money, power, and status. Sorry, but it just does not always work that way! I have been told many times, "Life is not fair!" Get over it!

It is unfortunate that we define ourselves by our job titles and responsibilities. If we are a vice president, or higher up in the hierarchy of success than a director or manager, we often begin to realize too late in life that it isn't the title or level of the job but the contribution we are making that really defines whether we feel good or not so good about what we're doing.

Most of us work hard to get the right titles for what we think we deserve in life. We want the vice presidency, we want to be the C-level executive, we want the presidency and to be at the top of the organization. We want to be known for our titles, that is, "I am president; I am vice president; I am director." We may even want to be known for making statements such as, "I made some contributions last year to the educational system of America" or "I worked on saving three lives last week from a car crash where I assisted in the rescue effort." No matter what, we definitely do not want to be known as a "failure" at what we do in life.

It is therefore an accurate statement that if we are not feeling good about what we are doing in terms of our titles, achievements, responsibilities, and the amount of money we're making, we can be very, very miserable. Also, if we are fired, terminated, let go, cut back, or if we are in a state of approaching retirement, job change, or just not sure where we're going; all of these situations can produce a state of extreme misery for the individual.

Happiness can be defined as doing something you enjoy doing every day. Think about it. If you are doing something you feel you are contributing to, if you are being recognized for your skills and knowledge, then you might be very happy. If you are just there to make some money, to get a title, to have control and power, you might very well find yourself being very, very miserable because those efforts do not seem to reward you or leave you feeling satisfied about what you're doing every day.

On a personal note, I can remember arguing with my boss that I needed the title "vice president" more than "director" if I was going to get the job done. I felt if I could tell people that I am a vice president of the company, they would respect me more and think more highly of me when dealing with me. I told my boss I could bring in more business and sales as a vice president than if I was just a director.

One could argue that I was right. I think most people would rather deal with a vice president, a senior vice president, or even the president of the company when they are doing business with that company. On the other hand, I knew deep down in my soul that I really, really wanted the title of vice president for status and recognition. I thought that would enhance my standing in society and I could tell my children I was a vice president, et cetera.

Titles are important, and we work hard to attain certain levels in an organization that indicate that the company is recognizing our skills and abilities. We feel good about being known as the vice president or the senior vice president. But we find the feeling short-lived because the title carries with it responsibilities that are not what we thought we were going to have when we got to that level. In fact, I knew a lot of vice presidents and presidents who were not pleased and really did not give a damn about the title after a few months in the job.

For example, an executive told me that she had become senior vice president after twenty-one years of working to get that title. She also said that the title was almost meaningless, and she did not feel any different because she had been working for so long in the organization that many people had already thought she was a high-ranking officer. They did not know that she was not even a vice president until around ten years ago. Hence, she was very depressed that she had finally gotten the title that it took her so long to get and still, she found herself wanting!

Her case is not isolated. A major news network recently reported in a "Lifestyles" segment that studies conducted by several major universities indicated that individuals will be happier if they make $95,000 or less a year. Those who made less than $95,000 felt "free" and more in touch with a balanced lifestyle. The rap song, "Mo' money means mo' problems" may be true.

Miserable Bitches and Bastards

Chapter VIII

Miserable Bitches and Bastards

Chapter VIII:
Is the Price of Success Too High? What Is Too High?

As we climb the ladder of success, it becomes very apparent to most of us that there are aspects of any job that can really drive us crazy. All of the issues that are brought to bear here are from direct experiences I have had with individual leaders. One of the first challenges that comes to mind is when someone comes to me and says, "I know I'm getting there, but I don't know exactly where 'there' is. If I am the chairman and CEO, I ask myself daily, 'Where are my kids?' 'When was the last time my wife and I had dinner?' 'When was the last time I really enjoyed relaxing instead of worrying about the business?' 'When have I really attended to other people's needs, rather than attended to the company's requirements that I experience every day?'" Okay, are you asking yourself some of these same questions?

Many young people today are admitting they are not asking these questions. So are they, too, destined to pay the price? During the 1970s and '80s we stressed the word "balance" to assist leaders and achievers in finding a sense of equilibrium in what they were doing. All of us want to have time to be with our children, to be with our parents, to participate in community affairs, or maybe take the wife or husband or significant other out to dinner now and again.

One gentleman I was counseling said he could not remember what a balanced life could be. He mentioned that he never really had a balanced life! He was always after the gold and recognition by others. This drive for success kept him out of balance for thirty years. It also made him very wealthy and a man of "huge reach" when it comes to having an impact on our society. He is quite famous in the corporate world and has even written several books on how to "lead" a company. Privately, he admits he hasn't achieved anywhere near what he thought he would in terms of assisting his family, being part of the neighborhood, and having a few moments of enjoyment playing golf with

Miserable Bitches and Bastards

his close friends. All of these activities have eluded him for quite some time. Hence, he is a very miserable person when he speaks about his personal life.

Another aspect of moving up, as mentioned before, is the relationship of money and love. I once sat with a man who told me his life was miserable, but he made $20 million that year, adding to the $100 million he had already put in the bank! I said, "My goodness, that has to make you feel very good." He said, "No." It did not even register on his "feeling good scale" because he was having tremendous problems with his marriage and had a son who was addicted to drugs. Another son said he did not want to go to college, and the man had a daughter who was quite young and who was seemingly missing out on family support and protection.

He confessed to me he was "not" going to get a divorce and give his ex-wife half of his wealth, which at the time amounted to $50 million. "I'm not going to give that bitch half of the money I've worked hard to get." At one point, I told him he should give his wife half of his money and be done with it. His response was, "You don't live the way I do." And he was right. I don't live the way he lived. He had three homes, six country club memberships, and a whole lot of travel around the world.

Then, about six weeks into our counseling relationship, he told me he was diagnosed with incurable brain cancer. While in the hospital, his dialogue with me was around how he never got paid enough, that the money that he did have was nothing compared with what he deserved, and that money was very much how he measured his life and success. He would actually say, "I value my life based on the amount of money I have in the bank."

A final note on the subject worth remembering: Being miserable often drags those who love you and are around you down into the misery pit with you. The old adage about loving yourself first seems to apply. Get yourself out of the pit and you might bring many colleagues, loved ones, and family members out of the pit with you,

My Money Is *My* Money

The previously mentioned $50 million man somewhere missed the idea of wellness in his children, the success of his marriage, and the all-around "growing up" challenges that we all face. He kept saying to me that he was never paid enough. He actually laughed and said, "Paid too much? Who are you kidding? You are never paid enough for what you do." About a week before he passed, I was sitting with him and as I was shaking his hand and holding onto it, he said, "I'm going to die soon, I know it." He looked out the window of his hospital room with tears in his eyes. "And now the bitch is going to get all my money!"

Toward the end, as I was sitting next to him on his deathbed, he confessed to me that I had been right. That he should have given his wife half of his money so that he could be free to start a new life, free of the burdens of a failed marriage. On top of it all, he had a mistress whose life was equally destroyed after his death. The sadness of this story is beyond belief.

Power versus Powerless

Another subject that all of us have had to deal with as we have tried to make it up the ladder of success is what constitutes and defines power. So many leaders have told me that once they have attained the highest level possible they actually feel "powerless." At the request of the board of a very large corporation, I was retained to counsel the new CEO as he began to assimilate himself into the role of the new leader. I spent a great deal of time with him, and as I got to know him, he admitted to me that he wanted to be a change agent. He thought he would have the power to bring about many changes that were necessary to make the company more successful.

On the contrary, six months later he explained that he felt powerless and that he could trust no one to hear and know about his inner thoughts about how the changes should occur. This was because his direct reports within the company would soon tell others how "crazy he was," and what he was about to do. He found out that he could not even trust his administrative assistant to keep the confidences necessary to get things done.

Miserable Bitches and Bastards

As we worked together over a period of time, he kept lamenting that he felt that his efforts and organization would fail because he could not create the change he wanted, and he believed it was his fault. As it turns out, he was right. He had a tendency to order change to occur, rather than to build consensus and a vision about why change should occur. In the end, he set the vision and began to let subordinates think and contribute on their own, and slowly they recognized his personal change ideas were for the good of the organization.

1. Managing the Company/Organization and/or Other Lies

Another myth that we often tell ourselves while climbing the career ladder is that we are going to manage given situations, tell everybody what to do, and get things done rapidly. We are not saying that vision of where the organization should be going is not necessary. On the contrary, the vision needs to be set and agreed to by the top management team. However, it should not just be the vision of the leader per se. It has to be the "shared vision" of the team that is going to bring the organization into the future in a successful manner.

Far too often, leaders think that they have to manage the company and, in that scope or way of thinking, the responsibility to get everything done falls on them, which can create an extremely miserable situation. Eventually, the leader realizes the vision can get done only through his or her team. One of the basic teachings we give in our consultancy with top leaders is that when they start believing their "own press kits," they are in trouble.

After working with more than two hundred men and women who held the titles of CEO, president, or chairman in their respective organizations, I observed that the majority clearly claimed they felt they were in the most powerless positions in their companies or organizations. Almost all felt that they had assumed—at least in "their" minds—that once they had made it to a leadership position, they would be managing the company. They believed they would be held responsible for the business failures, and they knew they were highly overpaid by everyone else's estimation. But they would still be responsible for managing, looking after, and directing the company in the right direction.

One can certainly debate this dilemma, but often the lonely, powerless feeling caused those individuals to feel a sense of failure that they could not describe to other people. No one would accept that a CEO had tried to tell me he had failed. Think of it this way: he worked most of his life to at least get a certain title, position, or role, and he still finds that he is not really directing the organization. One chairman of a $42 billion company told me, in fact, that he often sent three or four people on the same assignment just to make sure it actually got done, because he did not have the confidence that any one of them could get it done alone.

Even with his direction, most of the time the individuals failed. However, the chairman would often find that one individual did the job a little better than the other, so that he would frequently send them all on the same assignment hoping that something would be accomplished. The board of directors eventually discovered this management practice that the chairman used, and the board hired me to correct him. The principal reason I was hired is because the chairman was wasting a lot of executives' time and was actually held in disregard by his own subordinates. The subordinates begin to compare assignments and the CEO was in real trouble when that happened.

It seemed that the breakthrough in this case was that the chairman soon learned that he too was a servant of the company and that he needed to entrust others to get things done in a state of consensus and agreement on the direction of the company.

What I just stated is a huge mouthful of what sounds like baloney, but it is often called today's "servant leadership," which we will be examining later in this book. It is one of the answers to getting out of a state of being miserable, and perhaps in its own right, it is the only answer about escaping being miserable in the top position. A leader serves his or her subordinates; not the other way around.

In other words, the board says you have the job of being the boss. You can accept that and think you have total responsibility for telling the company what to do, unless, of course, the company fails. All of these factors can make you miserable as well. The reason why you are paid "the big bucks" is to be

Miserable Bitches and Bastards

the leader. You are paid the big bucks because you are the big person who is going to get the big project done at all costs.

In summary, as leaders, we often remind ourselves that we are the boss and we have to get it all done. In many cases, people take on that responsibility because they take it very seriously. Huge stress levels mount on the executives and they often feel so lonely, so unsupported, and so misunderstood that they can be mentally and physically affected to such a degree that they decide to leave the position. This kind of thinking about oneself and one's importance can actually lead to failure because it is narcissistic, and leaders begin to think more about themselves than they do about the business and those who can help it succeed.

One way of dealing with the pressures that come with leading and guiding business can be found in what consultants like to call ethics or values systems. Some firms like to call it "the way we do it at our company."

Our consulting company has assisted many companies in writing a code of ethics for their businesses. These codes were usually agreed to by the boards of directors, after being written by C-level executives in the hopes of having the "code" cascade down the organization through all levels of management. Take, for example, the statement: "We treat all customers with the utmost care and respect." When you look at it, it sounds very nice. But often there are plenty of situations when the business does not treat customers really well, or does not think of the customers' well-being, even though that statement is number one on the values statement. Many management teams are miserable because their companies' value statements are lies that everyone is trying to live with as they operate their business.

One of the more interesting activities that we used to do with executive teams was to write a new code of ethics, after they had examined their organization's existing code, to see what the differences might be between the new code of ethics and that from, say, twenty years ago. We did not stop there. We then asked each executive to write his or her own code of ethics and put it in a metal frame on their desks so that subordinates and clients could see what they stood for and their relationship with the overall corporate code of ethics. Yes, I have mine. You read about it in chapter IV, and you will find all the specifics there on page 41. But the point is, if you do not have one of your own codes of ethics, you should develop one right away. You will find it an interesting project. So will your friends, loved ones and subordinates.

It's a very interesting learning experience to have somebody talking about these kind of issues in order to get an agreed-upon statement that will represent management's attitudes about how they will operate the business in an ethical way. This kind of activity can create a lot of pressure, stress, and time spent debating certain words. But it is a digestive process of management because it appears every day, in every company, and it addresses whether management is doing the right things to build the business with ethical and supportive methodologies.

The reason this activity is recommended in this book is that many times the concept of greed, the need for success, and the expectation of making money overtake the overall social responsibility that the company has to produce services, products, and quality. These are all standards of expectations that have been created by the company itself, and our overall society is counting on a company to be what it says it is. Society expects organizations to be as honest and straightforward and as beneficial to the community as they possibly can. Anything less than that spirit destroys the trust of the population in the organization. Therefore, in the final analysis, I think we would all agree that all we have is our reputations at the end of the road. A reputation for a person or corporation is almost everything. If it is damaged or destroyed by mismanagement and unethical behavior on the part of the leader or the organization, the loss is immeasurable.

So all this represents a balance. As mentioned earlier, all that I have been writing about is to you, the reader, with the hope that I can assist you in gaining a sense of balance throughout all these pressures and challenges that can make you extremely miserable. No one has all the answers. And, in fact, most of us do not even have most of the questions we should be asking.

Miserable Bitches and Bastards

It is my philosophy that when you lie to yourself about anything, you are committing the greatest sin of all.

If you say you are not frightened and you are, you are a liar. If you say that you are not worried and you are, you are a fabricator. If you say you thought you knew something was wrong in the company and you knew for sure that was the case and you did not say something, you are a liar to yourself. Whether you realize it or not, you are also causing a tremendous amount of stress on yourself and the company, which creates a state of being very, very miserable.

In the last several decades, the word "balance" has taken a paramount position for all of us to strive for in our lives. Most of us feel we are out of balance; that we have to concentrate on something today and then tomorrow we have to concentrate on something else. And then we find out we have been concentrating in the wrong two areas for several days, and we feel we are "out of balance" or even "out of control."

For example, often we are not spending enough time with our children, we are not spending enough time with our spouses, we are not spending enough time with our subordinates, and then, we are out of balance because we are not taking care of ourselves: we are not exercising or we are drinking too much. (Am I describing you?) Which is why we seem to be always striving to get "in balance" where we feel we are hitting on all cylinders all the time.

We are not sure whether perfect balance can ever be attained! And we are not even sure that balance is the right goal. Will we ever achieve perfect balance in our lives? It is not likely, and I doubt any of us will end our lives by saying, "I was always in balance" or "I always felt I was on target" or "I thought I could walk the tightrope" or "I thought I could always stay in all zones at all times." This is almost ludicrous, yet we are seeing so many authors now writing about how to regain your balance, how to take care of the children appropriately, how to go to church when necessary, and so forth. No one who I have read seems to understand that balance is a target—it is something we should strive to achieve, knowing full well that it is a goal, not an "event."

It is clear to me that we should appreciate what we have accomplished when we have been totally honest with ourselves, rather than whether we have stayed in balance. Then we can brag about whether we have taken all the right steps, and navigated all the tightropes, or juggled all the endeavors at the same time. Balance may be a goal, but many of us talk about it with great interest and do not really "believe" it exists. I am one of those non believers.

2. Solutions, Please! I Know the Problem!

It seems to me it's always a gleeful moment when leaders learn that they can become a lot less miserable when they've got their teams around them thinking about the business and they are not thinking simply about what they themselves want. Actually, subordinates already know what their leaders want—success, expected sales growth, low turnover, and the creation of new markets and products, all done in a reasonable amount of time and with great acclaim about how wonderful the company is for the general community at large.

A very personal training trick for developing subordinates is when the leader does not act like he or she knows there is a problem. I would often say in my position as chairman that this would sometimes happen at a social event. And there is a setting where employees want to tell you there is a problem somewhere in the field or in an operation. Oftentimes it has to do with human involvement. Various departments may not be operating together. I started learning to turn that problem around by asking the "telling employee" for solutions. I would ask if they had talked to the people who were actually involved in the problem. Most times the individuals who brought the problem to my attention would admit to me that they had not explored any possible solutions with anyone. In fact, many of the people looked shocked that I had asked them if they had spoken to the individuals who they thought were creating or involved in the problem.

In most cases when problems were brought to me informally, and sometimes even formally in a meeting, I would turn it around and ask, "What do you think about solving it, and what are your suggested solutions?" I would say, "Don't bring me a problem that you don't have an answer for solving." Think it through to the best of your ability, and then offer it up to me personally or to the management team. Then I would offer it up to the team at large, and see if we could get the best minds working on a common problem together. This system or approach worked very well for me in our consulting company!

Most leaders fall into the trap of thinking they have to have the answers and their own egos get involved. In many cases, they did not have enough information to do a good job at solving the problem. We emphasized that that job of solving the problem belonged to the subordinates, and the job of the leader was to praise the people who solved the problem. It was not the leader's job to solve the problem alone. Vision and praise are two key actions for a leader to have and to do.

With change happening so quickly today, we need people who are as near to the problem as possible to understand what to do to make that problem go away. Far too often, the problem is passed upward and upward and upward, maybe with a few ideas of what to do about it. But, eventually it is laid at the desk of the leader, challenging him or her to answer the questions wrapped around the problem. They, in turn, often fall into the trap of being too far away and too lacking in knowledge to make a good decision about solving the problem. That whole endeavor can create a very miserable situation for all involved.

When you think about it, we are all being paid to solve problems. Every level of management and/or employee is there to make something better and better and better. Those endeavors usually come from facing more and more problems faster and faster!

So I ended up telling people to bring me solutions. I would often say, "If you bring me a problem, bring me a solution or solutions."

3. It Never Gets Done!

Another pressure point is that more than 80 percent of the executives I dealt with commented frequently that "projects, plans, operations never seems to get done." I might describe it differently! Some executives say it never seems to get done, or that it never seems to be accomplished on time. Hence, frustrations mount and leaders wonder if they have the right team addressing the major issues or if they've got the right resources on target.

It appears to be an extremely regular challenge for leadership to determine the speed with which something is supposed to get done. In almost all cases, the leader is frustrated, mainly because he or she had to report to the board or an analyst on some endeavor that never seemed to get accomplished. In most situations, in fact, it usually falls on the leader to explain why something is not getting done.

This is a big reason why so many leaders are miserable, particularly when they believe they are moving in the right direction. But it is hard to explain to those who are looking at us from above (the board, shareholders, and analysts) and who are asking what has gotten in the way of getting something done on time. This seems to be an albatross that hangs around a leader's neck and is extremely debilitating for their sense of well-being. Here again, honesty is the best approach in admitting to the company why you failed.

"I'm Not Your Mother or Father: You Make the Decision"

Another issue that is always frustrating for leadership is why subordinates will not make decisions. Many years ago, I had a leader at General Foods who complimented me one day and said, "At least you're not afraid to make a decision." I accepted the compliment, assuming it was one! When I thought about it carefully, he may have been thinking I make decisions too easily, and perhaps not as well thought out decisions as they should be.

Several top leaders have been quoted as saying making a decision is better than making no decision at all. I am not sure I agree with that overall statement because not making a decision—if you understand me—is making a decision. In other words, if you make a decision not to act and not to do anything at that moment, it is a decision. In any case, I have told people, "I'm not your mother or father; please tell me what you think we should do and you make the decision as to what that process is going to be."

A famous leader I know said she would rather see someone take a risk making a decision and then check to get everyone's consensus—which just is not going to happen. A leader is someone who has the vision and can gain the acceptance on the part of his or her subordinates that the vision is correct. Then the leader can sit back and watch people make decisions to go get something done.

Miserable Bitches and Bastards

Making a decision is showing your capabilities to understand the challenge and to take risks in meeting those challenges. I do not know of a single organization that is successful in life, as defined by both society and the organization itself, without taking risks. To take a risk you have to make a decision to do so.

By now, in reading this book, you have come to realize there are probably millions of ways and activities and pressure points that can make us very miserable in our lives. Most of what we have written is about working in an organization and dealing with everything we deal with every day. Other pressure points are created around the following questions:

- "Why don't many employees understand me?"
- Like with our children, we ask, "Why don't they listen to me?"
- To our subordinates, "Why don't they support me?"
- And when it comes to most colleagues and those around us at work, the questions are: "Why don't they come to me?" "Why do these people seem to ignore me?" "Why do I feel so alone?"

In reality, how many of us really feel we are understood, appreciated, supported, looked after, taken care of, or even liked in terms of who we are? Don't most of us worry about being alone, being underappreciated, being misunderstood, not being involved or asked to participate, or disrespected? All of these concerns are driven by the question of why people don't understand us. In three recent consulting assignments—two cases where these worries were strongly felt by CEOs and one by an owner of her own business—all felt they had explained their situations repeatedly but were not understood. They believed that people had purposely and with malice acted as if they did not understand what the individual leader was asking them to do.

In most cases, there is a responsibility on both sides—of the communicator and the "communicatees"—to understand one another. Often, styles of communications, styles of operation, and styles of leadership come into conflict. They can cause a breakdown in understanding. However, the basis of most of this particular state that exists between people is driven by some deeper emotions that may be, in fact, led by jealousy, greed, and personal dislikes.

Poor communications styles—such as when one person wants to talk about the past and someone else wants to talk about the future, or when one wants to talk about right now and another person wants to talk about getting more data—can destroy the team, the leader, and the organization. All of these various styles come to bear and can make the individual who is playing a leadership role feel extremely misunderstood. Styles can conflict and be a big reason why things are not getting done, and can be extremely frustrating, and a "production machine" of misery.

I am reminded of the time I was working with a leader of a $7 billion sales organization who told me that "the miserable bastards [his subordinates] just don't want to understand me." It seems that morning he had had a meeting with his staff and they all just stared at him because he told them what they were going to have to do to make things right for the organization. "They all stared at me with this dumb look on their faces," he said, and did not respond to his statement that "we better get our butts moving." I asked him why he thought they responded that way. He said, "I think they're all idiots." I responded, "All idiots?" He said, "Yes, including myself." I asked him why he included himself in that characterization and he said, "Because I hired almost all of them."

I asked him if he considered that maybe it wasn't the case that they did not understand him, but rather that they might be frightened of him, may not agree with him, and therefore could not respond. And since they did not respond, he thought they were idiots. "In other words, whether they were idiots or not, they're simply not responding to you, and they're basically saying they don't understand what you want them to do." He said, "Yes, what the hell does that mean?" I said, "You're doing it to me right now." He asked what I meant by that. I said, "You're staring at me and you're frightening me and you may think I'm an idiot because I don't understand all of this. Yet you're paying me to be your counselor, your consultant." Fear produces very little on a success chain except *more* fear.

Miserable Bitches and Bastards

Yes, we often hear athletes and theatrical performers telling us that the fear they felt prior to a performance or a big game is good because it produced higher energy and a greater sense of concentration. The studies indicate that fear may be good for short periods of time, but it can be extremely debilitating over longer periods of time. Enough fear in an organization can shut it down and make the organization say and do things that have absolutely nothing to do with the business other than trying to get out a state of the fear produced by management.

The same kind of principle works with children. In fact, it works for everyone, including spouses and friends. If you are constantly causing a state of fear, you're just going to get more fear in response. Pretty soon, you will find yourself totally alone with no supportive behavior, and no one will understand you. Remember what President Franklin Roosevelt said to a weary nation that was desperate to climb out of the Great Depression in 1933: "The only thing we have to fear is fear itself." When it comes to treating people in the workplace, it is so very true.

I am sure by now you understand the word "miserable" and how it applies to most human beings. Perhaps we have even overstated how one feels when one is miserable. Yes, there is the other side, real depression, where you are psychologically ill. However, the sense of being miserable seems to come and go with regularity and can become a way of life for someone trying to influence others and build a successful organization.

So I am sure you are asking yourself, "Okay, I know what the problem is, but how do I get out of the 'pit of misery'? Is there an answer? Or do I just have to live with it all my life?"

You may be familiar with Joel Olsteen, who uses the power of the scriptures and religion to be positive in his way of thinking, and says to a point that being miserable is a choice. You can decide to be positive and to live life on a daily basis and stop worrying about the future. He claims that God can take care of the future, and to worry about it just adds more stress in our lives. We really do not have much control over what is going to happen. But we do have a lot of control as to what is happening today and how often it affects your state of mind.

It sounds good, and I agree with Olsteen and others who say that we, as individuals, are basically in control of our own lives as to attitude and almost as to how it all works out in the end because of what we believe. For the remainder of this book you will read a great deal about servant leadership.

Whether you believe in the teachings of Christ, who set up a servant approach to his disciples and to the world, not only through his sacrifices but even in the act of washing the feet of his apostles at the Last Supper.

I believe when you are working with your subordinates and you are serving your family, employees, friends, and society that you have taken a huge step in the right direction of getting out of the misery pit. *It appears that when we are thinking of others and contributing to others, we might even want to say to others around us, "I'm the happiest I have felt in years" and "I feel good."* In fact, James Brown had a famous song by that title in 1964. Is it any wonder it was a top-selling hit? When was the last time you said, "I feel good"?

Miserable Bitches and Bastards

Chapter IX

Miserable Bitches and Bastards

Chapter IX:
Climbing Out of the Misery Pit:
Is There an Answer to
"How Do I Become Less Miserable or Even Become Happy?"
—Yes!

Is there an answer? Yes, there is an answer! Up to this point, we have been talking about being miserable and various examples of what we feel like when we are miserable.

Now let's change direction. Let's focus on how we climb our way out of the pit. To be sure, most of you who are reading this book by now are either feeling you've been in it, are still in it, have never been in it. But I bet you know people who have been miserable in the past or are currently still miserable.

The first step in getting out of the misery pit is to believe that you can do it. It seems so many people almost enjoy being miserable. Perhaps it is because they get more sympathy, when in reality, in the long term being a miserable person is extremely painful to the individual. It is, in fact, a good way to lose friends and/or loved ones tending to you. It is essential that we accept responsibility for our own miserable status. Far too often, we blame other people for the situations that are troubling us. We will discuss this challenge later in the book. But you must realize that you are the only person (individual) who can change your behavior enough to get out of the misery pit. You alone!

Second, we must recognize that this is not an event but a process that takes time to get right, and to accept responsibilities for our own state of mind. It takes time, just like exercising, to change the mind and/or change an attitude.

Miserable Bitches and Bastards

I know when I work out I feel better the next day. Sore muscles, yes. But I feel better. How about you? Do you feel better physically after you work out? The answer should be yes! However, I confess that the need to physically work out is a major attitudinal challenge that I have to face every time I think about going to the gymnasium and going through my workout routine. It does not come naturally. I would much rather read a book, go to dinner with some friends, or do almost anything but work out. (Other people actually enjoy working out.) Also, I wonder when people say that they are really outside the miserable pit, if they are really telling me the truth. Is it really fun to lift weights and run two or three miles on the treadmill? Can you truly say you enjoy it? I yield to anyone who say they can. And, I yield to those and admire those who do get off their butts and go do it.

It's the same thing with changing an attitude toward being miserable or not being miserable. The first thought is, "Oh, my goodness, I could have a serious illness, or my children aren't doing what they're supposed to be doing, or the weather looks ominous." Yet, all these points can be looked at differently. We need to approach life by thinking positively about our children and their activities; and how we are going to influence them to be even better in terms of what they're trying to do with their lives. The same thing about the weather. Bad weather comes, good weather comes, and it is not something we have control over. So why worry about it?

Finally, I think it is a conscious decision one makes to climb out of the misery pit and to start looking at the brighter side of life, such as saying, "I'm alive, I feel pretty good, I've got a good job, I've got a great family who loves me, and I've helped three or four people lately in some capacity." Yes, there are negative aspects of life that are all around us. However, concentrating on the negatives has us living in a negative state of mind. Worrying about death, health, and the well-being of others can make you extremely miserable. When you are miserable or worrying about others, or yourself, it is like experiencing death or poor health several times over.

I think there is a secret in trying to live moment to moment, rather than always thinking things will get better in the future. Of course, you can always think things will get worse in the future. In either case, adjusting to celebrating the moment, thinking of how well off we are at the time, even though we may be having some difficulties with our health or our jobs, we are, in fact, alive and that life gives us many opportunities to be positive and influence other individuals in helpful ways. In essence, staring at life as if it is just the moment that we have because that is the reality of the situation we all face. We really do not know if it is going to get better or worse in the future. Actually, we know it will do both!

The only thing we know with certainty is that we will expire at some point, and it is a frightening thought. However, we have the time left between that moment and now to deal with it. And, we can make a decision to be either positive or negative about our day-to-day living. It is not easy to change our way of thinking, but it is so good if we can do it. Engage and give to others to get over being negative.

One approach to becoming more positive and living for the moment is to always be open to learning. At least you can say, "I can relax and enjoy the moment," "I can celebrate my life," and so forth. Would it not be more beneficial to see yourself learning something you can work with the rest of your life; something that you will find enjoyable and maybe even be helpful to others?

You already know the theme of this book is being a servant to others; thinking of the other person rather than yourself. Recently, while working with an executive who told me he was down about everything in his life, I switched my hat from being a career guidance counselor to being a little more of a servant guidance counselor, in the hopes that he would realize how fortunate he was.

Already in life Joe was independently wealthy, had three lovely children, and had a wife whom he had struggled with, but she was putting up with a lot more than he was in terms of how they got along. He even admitted that to me personally. And yet, he couldn't find himself being positive about anything. His shareholders were negative. His employees were not performing, and his long-term view of the business, life, and the future was extremely negative. He often spoke about how bad things would be in ten

Miserable Bitches and Bastards

years, how our educational system is failing, and how the whole world is turning against America. He would go on and on and on, to a point that one day I asked him if there was anything in his life that was working out the way he thought it should be.

He looked at me for the longest moment and he said, "I really am negative, aren't I?"

I said, "You're off the charts, and you're only making yourself unhappy and more miserable each day as I work with you because we don't talk about how to get things done. We talk only about how miserable you are. It's almost becoming a waste of your time and mine because you don't want to look at things in a way that you can have some influence for good in the future."

He said, "Oh, you're just BS-ing me."

I looked at him and said, "No, I'm not. Think of it this way. Your entire company reflects you. Your own people are negative. You just said so. The board of directors is negative, not engaged, as you say. Your own life seems to be too busy for anyone to be involved with you. You just said that! Your children do not pay much attention to you because they are fearful of you. You just said that to me! You describe your own pit of misery. What would make you happy? What would make you feel good and not so miserable? Any ideas?"

An extremely long pause followed, and I think there was an emotional urge behind his eyes that made him appear to be almost tearful. Then he said the strangest thing. "People expect me to be miserable. I am what I am expected to be."

I said, "Let's try an experiment. Next time you are with your staff, start out by saying, 'What do you think is good about the business?'"

Joe looked at me and said, "Bill, they won't respond. There really isn't anything good about the business right now. We're negative in sales and negative in profits."

I asked, "Isn't there anything good about the business right now?"

He responded, "Bill, I don't know."

"What do you mean you don't know?" I asked. "You told me about these new services you're going to start offering in about a month. Isn't that a good thing? Won't that benefit the business?"

"Yes," he said. "That's true."

"Can't you get some optimism wrapped around that activity?" I asked. "If not, why do it?"

Joe stared at me for the longest moment.

I finally said, "The other day you told me that a person you knew at the company had done a really great job with a certain activity. How long did you spend complimenting him or her for that activity?"

His response to me was not surprising, "I didn't even tell him it was a good job."

"Why not?" I asked.

"Well, I expected him to do a good job," he said. "That's what they all get paid for."

"You know we work for recognition, praise, and results, not just money!" I replied.

Joe stared at me again and said, "I don't get it."

I said, "I know, that's why you're always miserable. Let's try walking over right now to that individual's office and sitting down with him to compliment him on how well he did on that particular project, even though it occurred two weeks ago."

He said, "You've got to be crazy."

Miserable Bitches and Bastards

"Why would you say that?" I asked.

"Because he's going to think I'm crazy."

"No, he won't," I replied. "He will love the feedback and will enjoy the moment of your recognizing how well he did. And, he will tell others that you did it!"

Well, of course, we walked over to the individual's office, and in a stammering way, Joe told this employee how much he appreciated what he had accomplished a couple of weeks ago, how he was looking forward to working with him on this project, and the tremendously positive impact it would have on the company.

For a moment, the employee, whose name was Mike, stood and stared. And then I thought Mike was going to give Joe a hug. Joe thought the same thing, as we walked away from Mike's office. Joe was in a state of euphoria. For the first time, he and Mike had bonded on this project, where before they had always been distant from each other.

I am sure as a reader you already know all of this, but I do not know if you practice it. You have all heard the old line "You get more with honey than with vinegar," as well as other old adages to that effect. They are true. People need to know they have done a good job not just for money or status, but they need to be told you are going to be there for them; that you will help them in the future on other projects. It is so imperative for the leader to be a contributor to individuals who are struggling to make it all happen.

Another miserable activity is being dogmatic. It is good that we can predict certain behaviors from people in our lives, responding certain ways and being comfortable with those responses. On the other hand, to be constantly thinking one way about the challenges of life can destroy our ability to learn and compromise with others.

It almost supports being miserable when one says, "I am this, I am that," such as a Republican, a Democrat, a Christian, a Muslim, a Mormon. When we continuously babble on about our beliefs without any willingness to change, or learn, adapt, or move to a different position, it is dogmatic and limiting. And it's "destructive" to the aspect of embracing change.

To be sure, we all have guidelines that we were given as children through our parents, our religious beliefs, society at large, and even from our laws, which are handed down from our local, state, and federal governments and teach us to think and behave in certain ways.

I do not think anyone would disagree that we are only as strong and as safe as our neighbors. Yes, in the Bible we are told to treat our neighbors as we would want to be treated. I am often challenged by that thought because sometimes our neighbors may not care how we treat them. But, by and large, that statement is correct. Almost all of us want a better education and security for our children, health for our families, financial security for when we retire, and recognition that we've contributed to society, to our children, and to our loved ones.

There is a joy that occurs in the inner soul when we know we are contributing to society and helping it improve. Even if it is just counseling one girl or boy, one family, one husband or wife, one daughter or son. If we know we are contributing to their lives and being beneficial, helpful, and sensitive to the needs that surround us, then it is all worth it. You know when this happens!

Miserable Bitches and Bastards

Chapter X

Miserable Bitches and Bastards

Chapter X: Megan's Story—What Does It Mean to Be Successful?

Several years ago, I was asked to speak at an urban school in Harlem, New York, to children between the ages of eight and fourteen about career/life management and how to prepare for the workaday world. Yes, I know! They were very young to be thinking about jobs and careers. But the principal of the school was eager for me to get them thinking early on in life about what they would be when they grew up. As I was starting to lecture, since I am "so old and wise," they all raised their hands to ask questions. Unlike when I was kid, they had been taught to engage the speaker before the speaker engaged them. Not a bad idea!

I recognized one young man who was twelve and whose name was Paul. Paul asked how much money I made—a very personal and hard-hitting question to ask a guest speaker. I thought I would catch him by turning the question back to him! "I will tell you the amount of money I make, I said, if you will tell me that's how you measure success in life." Of course, I thought I had him! He surprised me by saying, "I'll tell you what success in life is. It's living in Westchester County (one of the richest counties in the United States), making $300,000 a year, living in a five-bedroom house, and being married with a couple of children."

While looking at him, I must admit I could not come up at that moment with a better definition. Living in the bigger house, having the bigger car, with a bigger expense account and salary, and having a happy marriage and family is the American Dream. Yet there were still 199 hands raised in the air waiting to be recognized so they could answer the question "How do you measure success?"

Finally, I saw a young woman—very small in size—with her hand up in a timid fashion. So I thought I might get some relief by recognizing her and asking what she thought success was. Her name was Megan, and I will forever remember her as the oracle for life. When I looked at her and said, "Megan, tell me what you think success is," she put her hand down and sat down in her chair. I had to get down on one knee because she was so short (I am six foot four), and I asked her to please tell me what she thought success was. At the time, Megan was just eight years old. When she then stood up, the other kids jeered her, claiming, "She never says anything." They assumed she was too new, too young, and too little to offer anything.

In a very shy voice, she said, "Success is making a contribution to others." Well, you can imagine as soon as she said her definition, everyone in the room just looked at her, all the other hands went down, and the teacher sat in her chair. I got down on both knees and then she said much louder, "I think the most successful thing in life is to be happy about what you do every day." Now, we were all hanging our heads, including me, and I asked, "Where did you learn these very insightful ideas?" She said, "I've always felt as long as I can remember that helping other people and feeling good about yourself every day would be what I would think is successful."

Megan's story is the "core" of this book, and the only way out of the misery pit that I know. It is not so much a story as it is an answer to getting out of the misery. Using her example, recovery starts by not thinking of yourself every five seconds, but thinking of others in a rational and supportive way. For example, recently I went through some very scary health problems and I found myself talking all the time to friends and relatives about myself and the health challenges I was facing. I began to realize that I was not thinking of others, but only of myself on a day-to-day basis, and I was getting more and more miserable than even my health concerns should have caused me to be.

It is a proven fact that the more we think and worry about ourselves, the more consumed we become in self-analysis. Eventually, we lose awareness of others who may have greater needs than our own. I say this only because so much of life is self-centered. Megan had the right idea of helping others not for her own gain, but to get outside the personal issues that often overwhelm us. Her comments encourage us to realize that we have brothers, sisters, neighbors, and friends in the world who are in greater need than we can possibly imagine. Any newscast will confirm this point!

Thinking about others and what we can do to provide assistance, insight, or support to those around us, takes the pressure off us as individuals. This requires shifting our points of emphasis in life. We will become more at ease, less miserable, and more worthy of praise from others. In fact, we will actually be fulfilling the concept of being of benefit to others, which makes a society a success or a failure.

After all, when people in a country come together to embrace a philosophy, a way of thinking, and freedoms such as we have in America, it can be extremely beneficial to the whole world. When you think about it, most of the world tries to copy America and the success that we have had in terms of attracting the best, the brightest, and hardest working people. The American Dream has long been a drawing card for people from other countries who want to come here and experience what the average American citizen experiences.

The other day I opened up Time magazine and I saw a story and pictures about refugees struggling to get into a boat. I saw a mother and a baby in one picture and then in another, it looked like the woman was drowning after throwing her baby into the boat. Thank God, most of us in this country will never know that kind of misery. But the reality is there are millions of people around the world who are struggling just to survive. I'm not saying we should ignore our own situations, but once we get outside of ourselves and truly care about others, it's amazing how blessed we will feel when we know we are contributing to the welfare of others, and not concentrating solely on our own problems.

My thought on this is if we do not feel the pain of others tugging at us when it is right in front of us, perhaps we are already spiritually dead. If we do not feel anything about others, we should start thinking about how to conjure up these feelings because they are what make us feel alive. I am not saying that if we are experiencing these feelings we are better than anyone else is. But once we experience them, we'll be much more aware of how precious and fragile life is. We will appreciate how important it is to hear a bird sing, have a nice cup of coffee, visit someone in a hospital, or speak with a colleague who is

Miserable Bitches and Bastards

struggling with his or her career. We will come to realize just how important it is to feel a commonality with humanity and that we can contribute even by listening and feeling the needs of others.

One day, while playing golf with an eighty-six-year-old friend, I noticed what I thought was a "perfect" moment. It was warm but comfortable. Here we were, two lifelong friends, our golf scores were even (I had to give him a stroke a hole), the sun was setting, and we had just hit two good golf shots in a row. I stopped the cart and I asked my friend if he thought it was a perfect moment as well. "I agree!" he shouted. We sat there for about five minutes in and it was just a perfect moment in time. Have you had any perfect moments lately?

As stated before, Megan mentioned the importance of being happy in what we do every day. I totally believe that anyone who feels this way should recognize it, repeat it to others, and affirm that feeling of being successful in life. Haven't you met a lot of people who claim not to be happy in what they do every day? Are you one of them? How many people do you know who dread going to work every day? It is not because work is so difficult, it is because work is so boring, or doesn't involve other people, or doesn't allow them to contribute to their organization. Many feel turned off or burned out. How about you?

Years ago, I wrote a book called Silent Sabotage. The theme of the book is that organizations that do not appreciate their employees will eventually suffer from "silent sabotage." This is where employees believe management doesn't care about them and their contributions, especially after a downsizing. Sooner or later, the employees' feelings for the well-being of management and the organization wane. Pretty soon, the entire organization starts dissolving because employees are spending more time at the water cooler or on their handheld phones or on their computers, rather than paying attention to the business. Then the business begins to suffer greatly from a lack of attention and begins to fail.

I have always felt that Megan was a sage, an oracle at a tender age to all of us in the room that day. I have discussed her philosophy with so many people who find her thoughts to be extremely revealing. Some people have come to realize that they too are not sensitive to others and are not happy about what they do every day. If you are not engaged in assisting others, or able to see how your job or career contributes to society, and you're truly bored with what you do and you're not truly happy in going to work, then you should think about "changing" your career and/or your job. I feel it is a moral obligation that you get into a position to contribute and be positive about your life rather than being negative, negative, negative thinking and acting. Life is far too precious to waste! Right?

Megan's wisdom is even more amazing when you consider it in light of what we can do when we pull together as a country, organization, or team and act as a unifying force for good in the world. Even though we have weapons of mass destruction, we also have speed, support, vehicles, and first responders who can quickly save lives in very stressed areas of the world. We've seen over and over again how people in a community come together and help one another through the very, very tough times that accompany hurricanes, tornadoes, forest fires, tsunamis, and other moments of trauma in our lives caused by nature.

For you as an individual, I cannot think of a better way to get at improving your life's worth where you are feeling that you're doing something or making a contribution to your own company as a leader or as an employee. Getting outside yourself is a major accomplishment for good.

Megan's belief about being happy every day can be very difficult to actually put into practice. Part of it is attitudinal because some people seem to always be unhappy—it has become a way of life for them. But most of us have a choice about whether we are going to make it a good day or a bad day. Should we want to do something and don't get a chance to do it, we can explode and be negative and blame everyone else. Or we can take it on the chin and say, regardless of the circumstances, "I am choosing to be positive, and affirming my life rather than damning it and feeling that 'I'm always the loser.'" When we really analyze our lives, we know there are moments of adulation and moments of deflation. It is not always negative or positive. We do, however, have a choice about what we believe and how we act.

Miserable Bitches and Bastards

If you want to read a document that speaks well about this issue of being happy with what you do each day, consider the words of President Theodore Roosevelt, who wrote: "It is not the critic who counts; not the man who points out how the strong man stumbles, or where the doer of deeds could have done them better. The credit belongs to the man who is actually in the arena, whose face is marred by dust and sweat and blood; who strives valiantly; who errs, who comes short again and again, because there is no effort without error and shortcoming; but who does actually strive to do the deeds; who knows great enthusiasms, the great devotions; who spends himself in a worthy cause; who at the best knows in the end the triumph of high achievement, and who at the worst, if he fails, at least fails while daring greatly, so that his place shall never be with those cold and timid souls who neither know victory nor defeat."

Megan and a much older Roosevelt discovered the formula for being successful. You have to care about others and be involved out there every day, despite the ups and downs. This way you can at least say you have felt good and that you were contributing to others while you were attempting to do something that was not necessarily self-serving and, in fact, contributed to the well-being of others. Those feelings are priceless, and they represent the real point of successful living. Trying and trying again and again is so superior to sitting on your butt and complaining.

In summary, it is easy to write about being happy and making contributions. However, we all know it is hard to do it and to assist others on a daily basis when we are all so focused on surviving ourselves. I do not want to appear naïve because your "own" economic security is critical, and no job is perfect. We all have up days and down days in our lives. But, if we can affirm that we need to contribute more and more to others, and to look at the good parts of what we do in our work and our careers, then we will feel much better as we continue to get out of the misery pit. In fact, I cannot think of any other way to escape our misery than by concentrating on these critical thoughts from Megan and Teddy Roosevelt.

We all should take Megan's advice to heart and use all the resources we have to create an environment within which we can be happy about what we are doing and content about where we are spending our time.

Okay, please take a moment right now and think about what you can do to stop being miserable. Come on and "think." Try these suggestions:

1. Say good morning to others and mean it.
2. Identify the one good thing you have done each day.
3. Tell your children or grandchildren you love them. Listen first before offering guidance.
4. Counsel a friend who is facing serious problems.
5. Give a dollar or more to the needy or contribute to your favorite charity.
6. Thank your boss, your fellow workers, spouse, and friends for being who they are and being so close to you.

Try it. Why not? Engage!

Miserable Bitches and Bastards

Chapter XI

Miserable Bitches and Bastards

Chapter XI:
The "Click" of the Moment

The moment we start worrying about ourselves is when we become focused on being wealthy, being seen as successful, being recognized for our talents, and being sought after for our opinions. All may be okay in the sense of the regular definitions of success but it can leave us wanting to be in a position to impact other people.

Having been a teacher, I recall that some of the most successful moments in my life were whenever I saw a child, all of a sudden, "get it." There was a "click" and a sense of connection with that student and with myself. It is an unparalleled feeling of success, and the same can be said when it comes to running a business. When you find your people getting it, marching forward on their own and going after the agreed-upon goals with enthusiasm, dedication, and purpose, it is amazing. There is a "click" in employees that occurs here as well as with leadership and it is unparalleled. Of course, the "click" occurs with our children and our friends and there is no emotion comparable when describing success. The "click" is success in almost every sense of the definition.

Perhaps Megan's story speaks to us at a very fundamental level because it represents more of an answer to a problem via a desired state of thinking. Part of the "wisdom" of her wisdom is that she does not tell us how to achieve happiness. She leaves that up to us to achieve and to enjoy the process.

Get Off Your Butt and Do Something

As I mentioned before, it sounds easy to be happy every day: take care of others and contribute to other people. But, to really do something, you have to resolve in your mind that this is an answer—to do something, to get out, to get involved, to take risks, to live in the moment, and not to worry about the past or the future. Think of the moment that you are in. Yes, we recommend planning and thinking of others, and the necessary skills you need to contribute to society. All in all, it takes fortitude and the personal decision to be in the moment and to serve others, and to really get outside your "being" and recognize the thrill of giving versus taking.

Miserable Bitches and Bastards

I think you know what I mean. Most of our society says: be number one, think for yourself, you are responsible for everything, you have to have the answer, and you have to do this and you have to do that. It is all somewhat true. But on the other hand, to blame others, and to live in a selfish fashion, where you are always thinking of your possessions and your level of income, you will hang in a very miserable state of being. It is easy to write these words, but it's very hard to live them in such a way that makes you realize how wonderful it is to contribute, participate, and to be involved in a loving, nurturing, and serving role.

Just try these small steps:

1. Ask your son or daughter or any young person what he or she thinks about the current political situation, and let them talk. Do not interrupt them. Do not feel that you have to instruct them. Do praise them for thinking and responding.

2. Trust and support your assistant. Ask how he or she feels the business is being run. Ask how the business can do better or what it can do differently. Listen to them; do not interrupt or argue with them. Ask for clarification and how to continue the dialogue, and do not do it on just one occasion.

3. Make a list of people you could engage with and solicit their opinions. Take care to avoid being an argumentative person who wants to show them how smart you are by disagreeing with them.

4. Make a list of subjects you would like to know more about and prioritize them so you can start searching for literature or experts on the topics. This is an effort to get you out of your boring, day-to-day routine. Most of us are bored at different times during our lives. And some of us are bored most of the time with others and ourselves. It is our job to get out of that part of the misery pit and become curious about what life holds and the mysteries that exist in this wonderful world of ours.

5. Join a nonprofit foundation, not just to give money to but also to actually participate in and to talk to those who need your help. Be a participant, not just a supporter, and see how you feel.

Chapter XII

Miserable Bitches and Bastards

Chapter XII: No Dogmatic Thinking

When you look up the definition of "dogmatic," you find "inflexible opinions of an individual." If you carry this way of thinking to a bigger scope in life, you find people saying, "I'm a Democrat," "I'm a Republican," "I'm a liberal," "I'm a Christian," "I'm a Jew," "I'm Muslim," "I'm Hindu," "I'm from the Midwest," "I'm from the South," or whatever, to a point of absurdity.

Often times, these descriptions indicate that a person is very inflexible about learning from or associating with others in a contributing way. To be happy in life and get out of a miserable state that you might be in, please examine the word "compromise." Somehow, that word has become evil in our society; that we would compromise our opinions or compromise our way of thinking. If education teaches us anything it is to be more open to others' ideas, and together with our ideas, we can progress as a society. However, if we stay opinionated, locked in, locked down, and remain dogmatic our entire lives, he will accomplish very little. Right now, America seems like it is so divided politically that we are in "Dogmatic Heaven."

It is shocking if you look at social media like Facebook; there you will find people every day stating "locked down" opinions that the president is "X" or "Y." Alternatively, that another person is "Y." And they actually state their opinions as if they were facts, or as if they truly know what has gone on, when they don't.

We need to explore, think, relate, and share our ideas as ideas, not dogmatic principles that are inflexible. History shows that flexibility has been key to humankind's progress in medicine, technology, and philosophies. Had it not been for people wanting to think "outside the box," no growth would have occurred. In other words, unless we reach out to opponents and find a common ground and a place where we can all survive together with our different opinions, we will all be going nowhere. "Wars" start at this point!

Miserable Bitches and Bastards

In all my years of counseling professionals, the most unhappy individuals were those who refused to be flexible and maintained that everyone had to think like they did. Unfortunately, they found the world extremely wanting because people did not agree with them on many issues. I asked one person I was counseling, "Do you really want a world without another point of view? Would you really want the only view to be Republican or Democrat and not have the other party to balance our thinking for the common good of us all?" I got a very, very nasty response.

The best example I can think of is a thirty-year friend of mine who is extremely liberal and dislikes anyone who is conservative. One day he was ranting and raving about how bad the conservatives are. His very rational wife said to me, "Bill, what are you thinking after hearing him complaining about how bad the conservatives are?" I hesitated for a moment and then said to my friend, "You're not going to like this because we've been friends for a long time, but you sound like a dogmatic conservative ranting and raving about how bad the liberals are."

I could not help thinking about John Kennedy's words, and how far we have come from his plea in 1958 to find common ground: "Let us not seek the Republican answer or the Democratic answer, but the right answer. Let us not seek to fix the blame for the past. Let us accept our own responsibility for the future."

Life is at best a compromise. We learn from each other and come up with a better answer. The old saying "two heads are better than one" is so true if we stand on principles, and the principles are pretty close. If you treat others the way you would like to be treated, it is pretty much agreed on by all members of our American government as a good way to work.

If we all stay in the same vein, or on the same track, we will destroy ourselves very quickly. So let's think in a way that's open and will allow us to learn from one another. It is very true that when you open your mouth and are talking all the time, you're not learning anything. I would add that you are also not paying attention to what is being given to you from someone else.

That truism definitely applies to us today, when you consider our political challenges and the threats of acts of mass destruction. We have to figure out a way to get people to feel included and know that it's not right to harm others. It has to start at a very early age, where parents are teaching children to serve and protect rather than take up arms and rip each other apart.

It starts by finding common ground, where we can all agree on a larger picture, such as good health, education, and success for our children and ourselves. So beware of dogmatic, repetitive, boring ways of thinking. If you want to get out of the misery pit, dogmatic thinking has to go, and we all have to replace it with positive efforts and outreach.

Quoting another Kennedy admonition, "Ask not what your country can do for you— ask what you can do for your country." Let's get up and move toward doing the best we can do for one another. It is very idealistic, I know, but very possible.

Miserable Bitches and Bastards

Chapter XIII

Miserable Bitches and Bastards

Chapter XIII:
To Serve "Is" One of the Answers—Servant Leadership

We have mentioned many times before in this book the notion of "servant leadership." We have also mentioned that there are many leaders who serve as examples of what true servant leadership means. The core of servant leadership is realizing you cannot get as much done by yourself as you can with others, and believing in another old saying, "What goes around comes around." You treat people poorly and they will treat you the same way.

Servant leadership is the answer to building an entire organization or specific team or even a successful family because it forces leaders to think and do what is best for the family or the business, and see ways that they can serve others in their lives.

A question we can all ask of others is "What can I do for you?" with a sense of "genuine" interest and support. Servant leadership is a way of building a successful organization and relationships. It starts by realizing any position of authority—whether it is a CEO or a manager, or even a general in the military—serves the people. When people feel you are looking after them, serving them, paying attention to their needs and wanting to assist them, you would be amazed at what will get done, compared with when people are frightened of you and afraid to tell you the truth or even what they are thinking.

One of my assignments involved working with a CEO of a $13 billion organization. She had pushed the company through tough times with her hardcore management style. However, the company was beginning to disintegrate in terms of talent loss, a loss of purpose, and more and more disapproval of the CEO's direction of the company. In fact, many employees openly wondered if they could attain the goals the CEO had set out. Subordinates began to lose confidence in their leader because she had put it all totally on

Miserable Bitches and Bastards

herself—she was going to be the one with all the answers. It was all about her!

I was hired when the company was several billion dollars off forecast worldwide and I was asked if I could help her focus on how to make the organization succeed. Of course, I took the assignment not because of my own ego but because I thought I could reach out to her sensitivities and her great sense of humor and have her build on those attributes. This would let other people see that she needed their support; she would use their ideas and their skills to take the company forward in a successful way.

When after five meetings I described what I was thinking to her, she said, "Frankly, I think you're crazy. The company has just run out of time. The company doesn't have a vision because we didn't invest properly in new products and services ten years ago. We're being beaten by competitors at almost every level. The only reason we exist today is because we have a great reputation and we're producing good and reliable products."

I asked her, "What is the number-one reason why the company has been successful?"

She answered immediately, "Having enough investment money to do what we needed to do."

I said, "Because of your investments, right?"

She said, "Yes."

I said, "Not according to all the books on management."

"What do you mean?" she asked.

I told her the management books all say the number-one reason why the company is successful is because of its reputation, its name, and the attainment of high-quality work in the past. Not just financial support, but reputation is the way to a successful future. Often consultants say the company ran out of money and then they failed.

She stared at me, thinking for a minute. "What's your point?" she asked.

I said, "You have a great reputation for introducing great products. How many new products do you have coming on line?" She said she did not know exactly. Her answer scared me. The CEO did not know what was coming on line in the current year.

I said, "You care about the company and you don't know the number of new products that are coming on line, and on top of it, I bet you don't know what impact each of those products will have in the marketplace."

She smiled and said, "I guess you know me well!"

"I'm going to make a suggestion," I said, "that you get your staff together, break them into groups, have them examine each of the new products, and see what they feel those new products will do as we approach and begin the new year. The second question for them is: How are we going to ensure that our company, the employees, and the new products will do what we say they will do?"

Finally, I suggested she conduct some studies of several customers who she could meet with personally and ask them about the new products and how they might feel about them. She said that had already been done by the firm's development team.

But I told her, "No, I'm talking about you going out and setting an example by talking to potential customers about the new products and asking about how you might adapt old products so that they are more usable."

She said, "I don't think that's my job."

To which I responded, "Isn't it your job to influence current customers and gain new customers?"

She paused for a while and said, "Maybe!"

Miserable Bitches and Bastards

"You came out of sales," I said. "That's how you got to be where you are. You knew your customers, you knew what they wanted and what they needed, and you brought this information back to the organization, and the organization produced the product that the customer wanted. Right now you're sitting in your office and you haven't been out of your office and out with customers in a very long period of time."

She smiled and said, "That's true. I didn't want to get in the way of our current sales team!"

I said, "I know you've been with your staff a lot lately, but all you do is tell them how bad everything is. That is called 'fear management.' It's not really helping anyone look at the future in such a way that they can see themselves contributing and succeeding."

A servant manager realizes that he or she works for his or her people, the customers, and for the greater good of all. Servant managers' jobs are to serve. They serve by asking questions, making decisions, and setting a vision. Using fear management never really works. It might help someone focus for a moment, but the fear can be so great that you lose the individuals thinking about the business and they become more concerned about covering their own butts. At this very moment if you are not a servant leader, you are hurting your company and losing the talent that you need most to succeed.

If you believe servant leadership is the type of leadership you want to embrace and use, I would recommend the following:

- Tell your staff you work for the company and you work for them and your intent is to assist them (and you are not a judge and jury). You also need to emphasize that you need to know how you can assist them in getting their jobs done. In other words, you should hold a "tone meeting" that lets them know that impressing you is not the important thing. The really important thing is getting the business done by impressing new and old customers.

- When I was a CEO at two different corporations, I held tone meetings. I said at one meeting, "When you come back from a client, I want to meet with you because at that moment you are the CEO-authority in our company about that business. What you found out from the client means everything to us as a company serving that client. If you've found out we've done something wrong and you are apprehensive because of my reaction, then you are hurting the business, you're hurting yourself, and you're really hurting me. Because that means you really don't trust me to listen to what the client is saying and therefore make the adjustments so that we don't lose that client or our ability to build a business with that client."

- Treat your people the same way you want to be treated. People who report to you work hard for the company and you need to listen to their points of view, how they feel about the business, and what they know about clients. It is a cascading program that can turn a company around in a very quick fashion.

- We have all heard about the "fear of management"; we have all experienced it, and perhaps been exposed to the belief that it will somehow suddenly turn the company around and make it grow. However, some studies now indicate these turnarounds, if they occur, begin to collapse because no one trusts management. And no one believes management has the company's best interests at heart. Think about it—if you have been constantly yelled at and criticized, you're not going to come forth with very many answers to a lot of touchy questions.

The great thing about servant leadership is when you hold meetings or make requests to do things, you are building trust and credibility, the building blocks that inspire and get things done. So many leaders hold meetings because of their egos, or because they want more data, or they want to show how powerful they are. All these games that companies and their leaders have played in the past have not, in reality, built the business.

Miserable Bitches and Bastards

Chapter XIV

Miserable Bitches and Bastards

William J. Morin

Chapter XIV: Yes, There Is an Answer

The answer is to understand that being miserable is not an event; it is a process of getting to a point where you think there is no hope for a better life. Just the other night, I was sitting with a man who admitted that after thirty-eight years of marriage he had decided to divorce his wife. I am sure you, as a reader of this book, understand that this act is awful. He is going to go through a miserable state and his wife will likely be in a terrible place, perhaps for the rest of her life. He also has three children who will be hurt.

He kept repeating over and over again how happy he was now, how much better he felt, and how much he wanted to embrace life again, compared with the way he was acting in his miserable marriage. I asked him what was so miserable about his marital state. He said that his wife was never happy, always negative, and she never agreed with him on what to do about getting out of the "pit of misery." He realized that he had spent almost half of his life hearing how negative, how bad, how evil life is. It had had a huge impact on him because he considered himself to be a positive person; someone who always saw new opportunities for growth and happiness. He was always brought down, from his point of view, by his wife's negativity. He also mentioned that he would "bring her up" and make her feel a little better but at the expense of his own well-being.

It should be noted that his children—a boy and two girls—grew up in this tense environment and began to recognize the loving, positive nature of their father. They started spending more and more time with him, and less with their negative mother.

I am sure by now you are thinking that these are everyday matters. But the point we want to make is he made the decision to change and get out of the pit. It took him several years to finally recognize that he could not stay any longer in a constant state of misery. This point is critical to all who have read this book. You have to make a decision if you want to get out of the pit

Miserable Bitches and Bastards

and escape from the shackles of feeling poorly and you have to decide to do something about it.

I did the very same thing this man did with changes I had to make in my own life. I have not looked back but, in fact, have looked forward because of the decisions to act rather than be acted upon. The first step in getting out of the pit is knowing that you are in it; that you are wallowing in misery. We are not talking about clinical depression or just the day-to-day happy or unhappy states that we all experience. We're talking about a period of time where you are really not pleased with what your life is all about.

In previous chapters, we looked at the concept of servant leadership as one way out of the pit—by serving others. Some may not be obligated to respond to you in any capacity, but you always know what the right thing to do is when it comes to treating other people fairly and with purpose.

Again, understanding that it is a process and not a momentary event is a big step. In essence, you set small goals, like you are going to talk to people differently, you are going to solicit advice, you are going to ask your spouse what will make him or her feel better, instead of asking, "Why aren't you feeling better?" You should even ask people what roles you should play to be a benefit to them, rather than anticipating or expecting them to change something for you.

This requires you to give time and energy to others and expect nothing in return for personal gain. The personal gain from servant leadership is internal to you. The payback is knowing you did the right thing and knowing that you served, rather than blaming others. You know that you did well because you received a simple smile from a child or a friend or even a homeless person.

Not long ago as I was recovering from some health issues, I found myself walking out of my rehab center on a rainy night and realized I did not have an umbrella. It was pouring and in five or six steps, I was drenched. I complained to myself about how mistreated I felt. Then I saw a man sitting in a wheelchair in the rain and I went over and pushed him under the overhang so he would be protected. He said, "Thank you very much," and just looked at me. The look was enough to satisfy my sense of well-being, and it impressed on me that I was still a very lucky person.

I turned the corner and continued to walk in the drenching rain, and realized that I was no longer getting soaked. I looked around and there was a man standing next to me holding an umbrella over my head. "You look like you could use some help," he said. This gentleman walked with me for two blocks in a rainstorm. I did not know his name, he did not ask me for money, and we didn't even shake hands. But I thanked him profusely. And he said to me, as we were walking up a hill, it was "the least I could do." I could tell that he felt better helping a drenched older gentleman, and I certainly felt better being a lot drier than I might have been without his help.

Plan to Change

Surprisingly enough, planning for change can be fun. You set small goals, such as visiting your kid's school, or visiting a loved one or friend who has been ill, even when you did not really think you could make it. You can reach out and serve through your church or nonprofit organization. Or you can write a book, a memoir, or a letter to each of your children and tell them how much you love them. Small steps begin to change your attitude. That is what we are saying it takes to get out of the pit—a change of attitude. The small changes can really make a difference. Reach out and ask people what they think. Don't state what you think but seek opinions and, if necessary, speak to a professional, like a psychologist or a psychiatrist or a guidance counselor, about your feelings and emotions. These professionals are there to help and assist you. Why not take advantage of what is available?

Another idea is to try something you have never done before. Travel to a new country, go to a new city, attend a new play or an opera, or study a language or music. Study, learn, and think. Do it to get outside of yourself.

A friend of mine who has been ill told me that one of the problems he was experiencing was his all-consuming focus on his illness. He said his only awareness had been centered on his pain and suffering, and not the pain and suffering of others. So he joined a Meals on Wheels program to serve food to others. Yes, he is now serving meals even as he feels the pain. But, he says, the pain is not as bad when he is serving.

Miserable Bitches and Bastards

I, too, recently had some serious surgery that ended well. But I found myself concentrating on me only and not concerning myself with others around me. That can become a habit, a way of life, because sometimes you need assistance from others at the hospital or from your family or friends. In times like these, you should let others serve you, and show your appreciation by recognizing how they are taking care of you. You can support them when they tell you about a certain problem they may have. In fact, while you are in the deep recesses of your pain and anguish, do not forget to ask them about their pain and anguish.

Finally, *reward yourself*. If you do something that seems trite but sparks a smile or love back from a grandchild, for example, or if you offer assistance to a student, or help someone get a job, or whatever it takes, "celebrate." Do not just take it lightly but also make it part of your plan to reward yourself for the goals you have accomplished.

As mentioned before, I recently went through a rehab program and never realized I had to set goals for even walking up a hill. I had to climb one staircase and rest, and then make it up to the next staircase and rest. Pretty soon I could make it without all the rest stops. Getting out of the pit, as noted previously, is a process. It took you a while to get into the pit. And it will take you a while to get out! But at least get started and have some fun building your plan—set some dates and goals, make a list of the people who may need your advice, help, or financial assistance, and get started. As noted in the previous chapter, get off your butt and get moving.

So with that goal in mind, here is my seven-point plan for climbing out of your own misery pit and attaining a life that is filled with a sense of accomplishment and an appreciation for being alive.

1. Have a passion for what you do: If you can, actually say you like what you do every day. To be sure, there will be days that are more difficult than others. But there will be fewer of those if you look for opportunities to do what you really love doing, rather than blaming life and other people for what you couldn't do.

2. Have friends with whom you can have true "give-and-take" dialogues and from whom you can obtain insights by having non-judgmental discussions.

3. Appreciate and accept the place where you live or change it. Getting up in the morning and feeling good about where you are and the people you are with are real advantages and keys to living a happier life.

4. Economic security is something we would all like. I'm not speaking about being overly wealthy where you have to worry about managing your wealth every day. But economic security means you're wealthy enough to live well, educate your children, help others, and help your family overall.

5. Have enough time to assist others, learn something new, teach something old, and do what you want to do, such as take a trip, attend a conference, visit a friend, or embrace that hobby you've never had time for, and have some fun.

6. Have a sense of humor. Attitude is everything and can make a huge difference in maintaining a sense of balance, happiness, and improving life. Optimists have a true advantage here. They see the silver lining in even the worst of situations and never let anything get them down for long. Complaining, on the other hand, can be deadly.

7. Finally, take care of your health. Use the knowledge that you have and are gaining each day about managing your health in a very positive way, and seek the advice of professionals so that you do not fall behind in looking after your own physical well-being.

At this point, I bet you're filled with some doubts, concerns, and maybe some disbeliefs. I hope some of my suggestions have "clicked" with you. My final wish is that as you practice not being miserable, you will experience joy, a greater sense of happiness and inner peace.

Miserable Bitches and Bastards

MISERABLE *Bitches* AND Bastards

I would like to acknowledge the following individuals whose invaluable contributions and assistance have helped make this book possible:

Maureen Sullivan: A brilliant writer, wonderful friend, and supporter who played a key role in getting this book finished and published.

Deborah Weiss Geline: A fantastic editor and proofreader who corrected so many of my editorial errors. I do not know how I would have completed the draft processing without her sharp eye.

Alison Josephs: An outstanding artist, designer and illustrator, who made this book look like it must be read.

Miserable Bitches and Bastards *William J. Morin*

The author continues with his interest in the following programs and endeavors.

The Advisorship™ — *Founder*

The Advisorship program provides a powerful solution to the isolation felt by CEOs and other senior leaders. CEO tenures are becoming increasingly nasty, brutish and short. Some sixty percent of today's Fortune 500 CEOs have held their jobs for six years or less, as stated in *The Wall Street Journal*.

WJM Associates™ — *Founder*

WJM was founded in 1996 by William J. Morin, an internationally renowned authority in leadership development. Today the company is led by President & CEO, Tim Morin, and a group of professionals with extensive industry experience and vision.

WJM is a recognized leader in providing high-impact practical solutions to companies seeking to achieve lasting and measurable improvement in the performance of their executives, teams and high-potential groups.

JobsyWobsy Prep — *Not-for-Profit* — *Supporter*

JobsyWobsy's mission focuses on youths, 10-18 years of age, and on attempting to lower the teen unemployment rate through targeted community outreach using digital technology to find and track meaningful work experience.

St. Labre Indian School — *Not-for-Profit* — *Supporter*

Member of the Benefit Society, keeping the miracle alive for our Native American children and believing that education changes lives.

Contact:
William J. Morin
bmorin@wjmassoc.com